THE AMERICAN DREAM SPEAKS
FROM THE PULPIT

"I came to Los Angeles from Cleveland about twelve years ago," Arsenio begins. "I came in a little tiny Pinto, with a beanbag chair and a crate of record albums. Reverend Murray here told me to hang in there. He said 'If it's for you, HE's going to give it to you.' So I hung in there, and whatever I am, I made it."

Stepping back from the microphone, Arsenio bows his head and begins to sob. The congregation is suddenly on its feet, clapping and yelling "Praise Jesus! Praise the Lord" as the organ music swells in the background. The Reverend Murray steps forward and drapes his arm around Arsenio's shoulder. Then, suddenly overcome with evangelical fervor, Arsenio rushes back to the microphone, stretches his arms to the heavens above, and shouts, "Belief in God can make anything possible! Don't ever give up FAITH! Don't ever give up HOPE! Don't ever give UP!"

The congregation goes wild. Bodies spill out into the aisle. Hugs, handshakes, and backslaps fill the air. In less than three years, Arsenio Hall has become the Great Black Hope—living, breathing, inspirational proof that the American Dream *is* within reach of all who seek it.

ARSENIO

The Prince of Late Night

An Unauthorized Biography

Aileen Joyce

HarperPaperbacks
A Division of HarperCollinsPublishers

HarperPaperbacks   *A Division of* HarperCollins*Publishers*
10 East 53rd Street, New York, N.Y. 10022

Cover photography by Darlene Hammond/Archive Photos

First printing: June 1993

Printed in the United States of America

HarperPaperbacks and colophon are trademarks of Harper-Collins*Publishers*

❖ 10 9 8 7 6 5 4 3 2 1

To Paula,
without whose research abilities and support
this book would not have been possible.

INTRODUCTION

INTRODUCTION

I t's 5:15 in the evening on a typical weekday. Stage
29 on the Paramount lot is bustling with activity as
the crew prepares for the nightly taping of "The
Arsenio Hall Show."

The studio audience is mostly a young and definitely varied MTV crowd—everything from right-
on punk to California surfer girls in Spandex body-
suits—a colorful, bobbing sea of Raiders jerseys,
leather jackets, short shorts, leopard halters, fuchsia
minis, and every type of hat imaginable, from purple porkpies to a Moroccan fez.

The set is alive with the sounds of chatter and
music as the audience alternately talks and listens to
the Posse, Arsenio's house band, which has been
offering a nonstop half hour of jazz and rock as an
energizing warm-up for their boss's entrance.

Backstage and out of sight, various crew members
make last-minute checks of the equipment. Oblivious to
the passersby, Arsenio is hunched down on one knee in
a private prayer off to one side of the curtain. It is a
nightly ritual from which he will soon emerge to dish

up another serving of "The Arsenio Hall Show" on Stage 29, where only four years before he had unhappily boogied to the sounds of "Solid Gold" as Marilyn McCoo's lively co-host.

Suddenly the band comes to a crashing halt. A hush falls over the audience as the band launches into the show's theme song and Burton Richardson announces: "And now, here's ARSENIOOOOOOO HALL!"

Hall emerges amid thunderous applause. He turns to the audience, bows slightly, then raises a clenched fist and rotates it in a circle. The crowd responds with the familiar barking chant: "Wooof! Wooof! Wooof!"

Arsenio races stage left and bounds up to band-leader Michael Wolff, whom he greets with an Arsenio-ized version of a high-five—a touching of index fingers, before bounding back to center stage for his brief opening monologue, which concludes with the yell, "Let's . . . get . . . BUSY!"

It is summer 1989. "The Arsenio Hall Show" has now been on the air less than eight months. And yet in that brief span of time, Arsenio has earned heavy marks for himself, and an equally heavy dent in the Nielsen ratings, as the first-ever black late-night talk-show host to grace American television.

Against all odds, with his all-gums smile, his flattop hairdo, lone earring, and colorful garb, Arsenio Hall has barked, insulted, talked, joked, flirted, and schmoozed his way into becoming the Prince of Late Night.

On this night, which could be any night, Sammy Davis, Jr., is a guest, talking about his career, his marriage, even his addictions—"I love booze!" Davis declares from out of nowhere. He follows this by asking an obviously surprised Arsenio if he could sing a song. Arsenio nods and the band tunes up as Davis moves from his chair to center stage.

When Davis is finished, he returns to his seat on the couch and, with an emotion-packed voice, looks at his host and then at the audience. "Arsenio," he says, "you're gonna be around a long time, man."

Arsenio, who only moments before had run the typical Hall gamut of being alternately sympathetic, irreverent, reverent, intense, and funny, appears to be sincerely touched, perhaps even a bit embarrassed. It is an arrestingly real moment in a medium composed mostly of unreal, often nearly surreal moments. And one of a multitude of reasons why "The Arsenio Hall Show" has proven to be the hottest late night show around since its January 3, 1989, debut.

"I think Arsenio can't miss," Davis later told a reporter, adding "He's so genuine. You can tell because nobody's envious. Everybody's rooting for him."

Davis was, at once, both right and wrong.

Arsenio has gone on to great heights as a TV talk show host, but not everybody has been rooting for him as he climbed the ladder of success. Arsenio's path to glory has been filled with fussing, fighting, and feuding, some of it justified, some of it nothing more than petty professional jealousy. But almost all of it created by Arsenio's inability to get a rein on his emotions and ego, and mostly his mouth.

Perhaps, as Davis perceived, Arsenio was "genuine" in those early heady days of stardom. But at some point along the road he was so successfully paving, Arsenio changed. He became a parody of himself, whether fawning over his celebrity guests or chastising a white America for being racist. Most of all, he became yet another example of the fact that power does corrupt.

Driven by a desperate need to "be someone" in a

world that is at best cold and unfeeling, Arsenio parlayed his vision of the American Dream into a multimillion dollar business. He succeeded in attaining fame and fortune far beyond his wildest dreams as a black child of poverty. And yet instead of discovering an inner peace, he has become even more driven by a recurring fear he cannot elude, no matter how fast or how far up the ladder of success he travels. It is an ever-present fear of failure, which, ironically, has only been magnified by his incredible success.

As Arsenio himself so tellingly explained not long ago: "You have a couple shows in a row where you're not funny, or a couple bad monologues, and you start thinking, 'I've lost it.' I don't want to go back to where I started. I'm happiest when I'm out there doing the show. The rest of the time I'm scared shitless."

As is often the case with celebrities whose lifelong dream turns into a reality, Arsenio joined the ranks of superstardom only to discover that despite the accouterments of fame and fortune, nothing had really changed, that he was still insecure, still struggling to believe in his own mind that he really was that *someone* millions of people believed he was.

"I guess we're a success," Arsenio once told staff members during the early days of the show, "but it doesn't feel like I thought it would."

Welcome to the world of show business. Welcome to the world of Arsenio Hall.

CHAPTER

1

I t's Sunday morning in Los Angeles, the city that never sleeps. Arsenio Hall is sitting quietly in a pew at the First African Methodist Evangelical Church in South Central Los Angeles, where the fires of spring 1992 are smoldering but have not yet been lighted. As the choir joyfully belts out a spirited gospel number, Arsenio happily bobs his head to the beat, seemingly unaware that other members of the congregation are staring at him.

The music ends on a high note, and the Reverend Cecil Murray moves to the pulpit. As he looks out at his parishioners his eyes fall on Arsenio and he flashes a mischievous grin. "Arsenio," he says, "come up here and say a few words."

Obviously reticent, Arsenio nonetheless extricates himself from the pew and dutifully approaches the altar, where he and Reverend Murray exchange hugs before Arsenio shyly steps up to the pulpit and the microphone.

"I came to Los Angeles from Cleveland about twelve years ago," he begins. "I came in a little tiny

Pinto, with a beanbag chair and a crate of record albums. Reverend Murray here told me to hang in there. He said 'If it's for you, HE's going to give it to you.' So I hung in there, and whatever I am, I made it."

Stepping back from the microphone, Arsenio bows his head and begins to sob. The congregation is suddenly on its feet, clapping and yelling "Praise Jesus! Praise the Lord" as the organ music swells in the background. The Reverend Murray steps forward and drapes his arm around Arsenio's shoulder. Then, suddenly overcome with evangelical fervor, Arsenio rushes back to the microphone, stretches his arms to the heavens above, and shouts, "Belief in God can make anything possible! Don't ever give up FAITH! Don't ever give up HOPE! Don't ever give UP!"

The congregation goes wild. Bodies spill out into the aisle. Hugs, handshakes, and backslaps fill the air. In less than three years, Arsenio Hall has become the Great Black Hope—living, breathing, inspirational proof that the American Dream *is* within reach of all who seek it.

If Arsenio seems comfortable within the walls of the AME Church, it's because he spent almost every Sunday of his childhood singing the praises of the Lord and praying for a better day. It's also because his father, as well as two of his uncles, were preachers. In fact, at one point Arsenio had seriously considered going into the ministry himself.

But then the Lord pointed him in another direction. At least that's how Arsenio sees it. He believes, as fervently as he believes in a Higher Being, that a career in the entertainment industry was his calling, his mission in life. He also knew, even as a small boy, that the odds of achieving his vision of the American Dream were so great it's doubtful any handicapper in the world would have laid odds on him. Yet through luck, determination, perseverance, and a talent to use and amuse, he made it happen, bigtime.

Church. Comedy. Faith. Hope. Determination. A flair for the dramatic. These are only a few of the components composing the complex personality of Arsenio Hall. He is a fascinating blend of humility and egotism. Without the latter, he would never have survived the nasty jungle at the bottom of the ladder to Tinseltown success. Without the former, he would be impossibly impudent.

Arsenio was born at 3:18 A.M. on February 12, 1956, at Mount Sinai Hospital in Cleveland, Ohio, the only child of Annie and Fred Hall, pastor of the Elizabeth Baptist Church. It was Annie who named their newborn son Arsenio after having heard the name twice in the nine months preceding his birth—once in the Bahamas and once on a plane—and believed it was an omen.

"Someone sitting next to her on the plane was reading a book on Greek mythology and told her it meant 'strong male,'" Arsenio explained. "Then a guy she met vacationing in the Bahamas said it was a great name, but he knew it as an Italian city, St. Arsenio." By 1988, Arsenio had added yet another interpretation of his name. He would then claim that his name meant "arson or fiery one" in Spanish.

Having been so creative in naming her only son, Annie Hall became the official creator of names for her family. According to Arsenio, she's now responsible for the names of four of his relatives. "You know how black parents are," he once joked. "They will just be looking out the window and see a car and they'll say, 'Le Toyota.'"

At the time of Arsenio's birth, his parents had been married for two years in what can only be described as an odd union of diverse souls. For reasons known only to her, twenty-one-year old Annie Martin, daughter of Oscar and Elizabeth Gamble Martin, had chosen to marry, on July 1, 1954, sixty-five-year old Fred Hall, a man forty-four-years her senior who had been wed (and widowed) twice before. Interestingly, the marriage certificate lists Annie as white, although Arsenio's birth certificate lists her as "Negro."

Whatever the reasons behind the marriage, it was an unhappy union from the beginning. And having a child did not make life in the Hall household any better. If anything, it made it worse. It was a stormy marriage, filled with angry bickering and violent outbursts.

"My father was a strict Baptist preacher and my mother was a wild and strong-willed young woman he shouldn't have married," he would later recall. "They fought over the most stupid, crazy things, and they fought a lot. It wasn't unusual for me to see my dad go for a gun during the arguments.

"My father liked gospel and Harry Belafonte, but my mom preferred the Top 40, and when I was little, I remember them fighting over the fact he was listening to a religious radio station, and she turned on the R & B station. It wasn't just screaming, either. It was much deeper, much more traumatic.

"One morning I was getting ready for school," he continued, "and my mother got into a fight with my father, and he reached for the gun he always kept on top of the refrigerator."

Surrounded by conflict, fearful of being abandoned, but unable to deal with an overwhelming sense of guilt that he was somehow at the root of his parents' problems, Arsenio spent a lot of those early years in bed, crying and wishing he had someone with whom he could share his fears, his loneliness, his pain. At one point the frightened little boy even went so far as to alternate sleeping in the top and bottom bunks of his bed, pretending he had an older brother who would protect him from the shouting of his angry father, the sobs of his weeping mother.

Shy and withdrawn, helpless to change the tenor of his life, Arsenio retreated from this hostile environment by turning increasingly inward. It is a life-long pattern, which still exists, except when he is either in front of a camera or an audience.

But no matter how hard he tried, Arsenio could not block out the unrelenting tension and violent arguments between his parents. He broke out in a series of unexplained rashes and often roamed the house in his sleep.

"I developed a rash and started sleepwalking. They'd find me in the garage in the morning, sleeping in the car," he once confessed. "Most people in Hollywood are in therapy," he added, "but not me. I was in therapy when I was five years old. I 'tripped' really hard over my parents fighting, watching my daddy chase my mother out of the house with a gun, watching her being beaten up by my father."

Mercifully for all concerned, Arsenio's parents finally separated. He still recalls the day it happened, even though he was only five years old, and barely in kindergarten, at the time. "I remember I was on my way home from school one day, and my mother drove up beside me in the car and said, 'Get in. We're going to Grandma's house.'"

When they arrived at the home of his maternal

grandmother, the by-then-widowed Elizabeth Martin,
Arsenio went into the house and discovered all of his
toys and clothes were there. Several months later, on
December 4, 1961, Fred Hall filed for divorce, charging his wife with "gross neglect of duty and extreme
cruelty." And eleven days after that Annie Hall
counter-filed a petition for divorce, as well as for temporary alimony and child support. She was subsequently granted eighteen dollars a week in alimony,
fifteen dollars a week in child support, and another
fifteen dollars for "unspecified" expenses.

After living only briefly with his grandmother,
Arsenio and his mother moved into a small apartment. Two years later, on February 11, 1963, the
divorce was granted after a bitter series of battles
which, at one point, had forced Annie Hall to file a
restraining order against her husband to prevent him
from making "disparaging, embarrassing, and humiliating remarks from his pulpit on Sunday mornings,
holding her up as an object of derision in front of
friends, relatives, and the general public."

When the divorce was finally granted, Annie was
awarded fifty dollars a week alimony for two years and
fifteen dollars per week for Arsenio's support, and Fred
Hall was ordered to pay for all necessary doctor, dental,
medical, and hospital bills, as well as "for all orthopedic
shoes required to be worn by the minor child."

A stenographer when she had married Fred Hall,
Annie found that her skills were rusty after almost ten
years of being a housewife. Determined to better herself, she went to school and supported herself and her
son by working several low-paying jobs. At that point,
what had become essentially a comfortable existence
became a struggle for both Arsenio and his mother.

"I'll never forget it," Arsenio said, referring to the

first apartment he and his mother shared. "I was sitting on the toilet and my feet were dangling down and a rat walked right under them. And I'm from the kind of neighborhood where the rats walk, they don't run. When I screamed, the rat looked up at me like I was in HIS bathroom.

"It's weird," he added, "because I decided right then, sitting there terrified out of my mind, that my big goal was to live in a house with no rats and roaches someday. Me and my mother. That's all I wanted."

With Annie Hall working and studying, trying to better herself and yet make ends meet, Arsenio spent most of his childhood being cared for by his grandmother and godmother. It was this experience, he would later claim, that left him with a self-professed high regard for women, and a general mistrust of men.

"I got shuttled around a lot and learned to take care of myself," he explained, adding, "I grew up real quick. Sometimes I'd have liked to have had a father around. Then I'd think about the only-child thing and I'd realize I'm the way I am now because of that. TV was my brother, and I sat there and planned the future."

The separation and subsequent divorce, which was granted in 1963, only a day before his seventh birthday, marked the beginning of a difficult time, financially, for Annie Hall, whose only skills were as a secretary, and a difficult time, emotionally, for her son.

"When they were divorced, my mom had a lot to catch up on. She was a housewife who had no skills and a lot of responsibility," Arsenio explained. "Five years later she had really developed as a person and made something of herself. But it took me walking around with a key around my neck and learning to cook and going after school to my grandma's and my godmother's. Whatever it took to get us through.

"Respect," he continued, "is seeing your mom work two jobs and go to school at night, and seeing her have to not eat so that I could eat, but me not knowing it because she made me believe she wasn't really hungry. You develop a respect for the strength of women in America. I understand women. I trust women. All I know is women. I'm surprised I didn't grow up to be a transvestite."

Arsenio dreaded the occasional times he would spend with his father, who was a strict disciplinarian compared with his more easy-going mother. The Reverend Hall, for example, always required young Arsenio to show up at the dinner table wearing a jacket and tie. Like a good Baptist, Southern synod of course, the good reverend also insisted there be no dancing in the house, something Arsenio could not fathom.

"I remember watching Chaka Khan on 'Soul Train,' which I just knew I would be on someday," he would later recall, "and my dad saw her and thought she was disgusting. He couldn't believe I wanted to be in show business, around women like that and liquor and drugs and stuff. He always wanted me to be a preacher."

Arsenio believes the reason he so revels in the freedom to walk around his Hollywood Hills home in his underwear as an adult is because of his oppressive childhood at the hands of his father. "I love the idea that I can sit at a table in my underwear and eat a lobster," he once confessed, "because I couldn't eat lobster and I couldn't wear my underwear outside of my bedroom when I was little."

So Arsenio and his father, who was old enough to be his grandfather, were never close, and not surprisingly, the visitations gradually diminished until the two rarely saw each other. "I was a mama's boy," Arsenio explained. "I didn't want to be away from her. So I didn't spend much time with my father. I'd see him at church on Sundays, because that was the church we attended. But that was about it."

Besides, the arguing between Fred and Annie Hall continued even after their separation and within hearing of their only son. "You think your dad has left both of you," Arsenio once confided to friends. "And then they argued about money a lot, too. If you hear these things, they fuck you up real bad.

"I overheard a conversation once when my mother told my dad, 'He needs tennis shoes.'

"And my dad said, 'Then why don't you have your boyfriend buy them?'

"It was one of those postdivorce arguments—my mother had a boyfriend—and he was punishing me. When that kind of stuff happens, it hurts. But I got over it—all the pain, all the negativity."

Later, long after he'd become an established Hollywood star, Arsenio would deeply regret the estrangement from his by-then-deceased father. "I don't think I ever told my father I loved him and I think I am a lot like him," he confided.

"We were both reclusive, both very hard on the 'L' word. I was a mama's boy and so it wasn't until I got older that I got to a place where I could love him," he explained. "When I was young, all I saw was him chasing her out of the house with a gun. I did not understand it and I didn't even try to. Now, if had the chance, I would ask my dad, 'Why couldn't you and Mom make it work?' This is an area that makes me very sad," he added. "I think I may be single today because of their divorce. I think, man, maybe I'm just afraid. I'm like Louie Anderson Lite. I need to write letters to my dad in his grave. I have a lot of unresolved shit in me."

Arsenio and his father remained estranged right up to Fred Hall's death on April 1, 1978. He was ninety years old at the time and had been the pastor of the Elizabeth Baptist Church for fifty-six years. He had begun as the minister of a small storefront church shortly after moving to Cleveland in 1923, and in those intervening years had seen his congregation more than quadruple.

"If I saw him today," Arsenio wistfully admitted not long ago, "I would say, 'Do you realize how much of everything I do has been influenced by you? From the way I wear clothes to the way I deliver jokes?' My father used to say, 'I want you to be a preacher.' But it's not up to you, you know. I'm from the school that says you have to be 'called' to preach."

Unlike his father and his uncles, Arsenio never received that "calling." However, he did find a lot of humor in watching and listening to them preach. "Baptist preachers are the greatest entertainers," he would later say with a laugh. "I used to be totally infatuated watching my dad preach.

"When I was little, I told him I wanted to be a preacher. But, well, I broke a few windows and had a few academic suspensions when I was in college," he confessed. "I found myself drunk on the lawn of a fraternity house more than once. I just didn't have the discipline. It's hard to be a good guy."

Arsenio's life following the divorce was disjointed and lonely. "Teachers would write on my report card, 'Arsenio needs attention. Is there anything you can do about it?,'" he recalled, explaining he believed it was that childhood feeling of aloneness that had created his interest in performing. "Yeah, I think it was a desire for attention."

And yet, as much as he needed the love and attention, he always seemed to be somewhere else, alone in a world of his own. "You couldn't get close to him," recalled Marjorie Banks, his Sunday-school teacher and the wife of Ernie Banks, the Chicago Cubs most valued player. "When you talked to him, he'd see you and yet he didn't see you. His mind was always on something else."

Arsenio grew up in blighted neighborhoods in the southeastern section of Cleveland. The seventy-ninth and Kinsman Road neighborhood, where he lived until his parent's divorce, was the kind of area where crime was an everyday occurrence. It was a ghetto then and it is a ghetto now. In fact, the building in which Arsenio lived on Crennell Avenue was one of the few tenements in the neighborhood that hadn't yet been burned to the ground, although his grandmother's home, which he regarded as his childhood home, ultimately burned in the biggest fire in Cleveland's history when Arsenio was away at college.

The neighborhood around Huff Street and East 120th, which was where Arsenio lived during his early teens, was equally downtrodden and rough. "When I think of my neighborhood, I always remember dry cleaner's plastic," Arsenio once said. "Everybody's windows had cleaner's plastic or some painter's plastic throw cloths. It was like, when windows got broken, they never were replaced."

And yet Annie Hall, who certainly was not blind to the troubles of the area, did her best to give Arsenio everything she could, including her love. "We lived comfortably on a minimum amount of money," she recalled not long ago. "The other people on the street

were hoodlums, but we couldn't stop him from playing with them. He had a very rich upbringing. He
didn't run with them in gangs. He played ball with
them, but he never allowed them in the house."

Instead, while most of his peers were into stealing
cars and snatching purses, Arsenio spent most of his
time practicing his magic act, playing his drum set,
and pretending to be an entertainer within the safe
confines of his grandmother's basement.

According to Annie Hall, Arsenio was always
busy, always into something. When he was six years
old, she recalled, he would make his own newspaper by cutting things out of the local newspaper
and then pasting them on sheets of paper. He even
made his own crossword puzzles, which he would
then pass out to the neighborhood kids, the same
kids to whom he paid pennies to deliver the *Cleveland Plaindealer*, pocketing the profits for himself.
"He really used those kids," Annie Hall said with a
laugh.

Arsenio also sang in the church choir, one of the
reasons he believes he managed to skirt the trouble
that abounded in the neighborhood, trouble that led
to the deaths of many of his childhood friends, one
of whom did become a transvestite.

Nevertheless, he still remembers the day one of
his next-door neighbors was shot and killed while
playing a game of touch football. He also remembers
the names of his childhood friends who are either
dead or in prison, as well as the next-door neighbor
who was shot during a pickup basketball game.

As for his high-school friends who fell victim to
their surroundings, Arsenio can still tick off their
names. "Von is dead, killed in a fight over a girl.
Weathersby is dead, killed in an argument over a

'last call' in a bar. Freddie's in jail. Jack was picked up for selling cocaine and hanged himself in the prison cell. Tyrone, the star basketball player, is in jail on two counts of murder. One day I realized, 'Yo, man,' nobody got out but you. . . ."

Arsenio's salvation was television. He spent hours in front of the family's nineteen-inch black-and-white Emerson television set, wearing a house key around his neck. But while the other neighborhood kids were watching cartoons and getting their late-afternoon dose of action-adventure shows, Arsenio was studying the on-camera machinations of Dinah Shore, who then had a popular NBC daytime talk show.

In fact, Arsenio now admits that his nightly trademark signature is based on Dinah's, which he practiced during seventh-grade study hall, much to the disgruntlement of his teachers. Later, much later, Eddie Murphy would express another kind of consternation upon seeing Arsenio's unique handiwork. "What the fuck is that?" Murphy asked as Arsenio signed an autograph with his distinctive flourish.

Nor were his viewing habits limited to daytime talk shows. His mother has recalled on numerous occasions how she would discover a light flowing out from under his bedroom door late at night. Flinging it open, she'd invariably find Arsenio, a lifelong night owl, transfixed by the late night chat-fests of Dick Cavett or Johnny Carson.

"I had a TV in my bedroom," Arsenio explained. "My mother would tuck me in at night and close the door, and I'd turn on the TV and watch Johnny. Then I'd try to listen to Larry King and some of the others. I had a thing for talk show hosts. Being an only child, I thought of them as my friends. I fell asleep listening to them.

"I remember once my mama called to me and asked, 'You watching Johnny Carson?' I said I wasn't. Then she saw that blue glow coming under the door and . . . She whipped me good. Not because I was watching Johnny, but because I lied."

Johnny Carson was then, and remains today, Arsenio's idol and his undeclared mentor. "All the kids wanted to be like Jim Brown," fullback for the Cleveland Browns, he recalled with a laugh. "But I wanted to be some little old white guy. I didn't think as a black man. I was living in the right time." Ironically, years later, after he'd achieved his sought-after stardom, Arsenio would find himself harshly criticized by various members of the black community for resembling, at least in their eyes, that "little old white man." "Uncle Tom," they would disparagingly call him.

As a child, however, Arsenio was not caught up in the negativity that would later surround him as an adult. It didn't matter to him that Johnny Carson was white. He could have been purple, for all he cared. All Arsenio knew was that Carson was the human embodiment of all that he aspired to be when he grew up.

So he would set up chairs in his grandmother's basement and pretend he was Carson, whom he has repeatedly identified as "the architect of all my dreams."

"To me, Johnny had the best job in the world," Arsenio explained. "He was what I wanted to be. He was funny in his own right, yet he was also a vehicle for movie stars and musicians. They all had to come his way, and he could make them or break them. Carson became such a part of my life that at one time I literally thought he would call me to take over the "Tonight Show" when he wanted time off. I was nuts.

"I admired everything about him," he continued, adding, "even the way he dressed. He had his own clothing company and one year was named the best-dressed man in America. Therefore, my dream was to become one of the top-ten best-dressed men in the country."

Thus, when Arsenio was old enough to require a suit, Annie Hall told him she would buy him something from Carson's line of men's fashions. And she did—"It was plaid, with bell-bottom trousers, and lapels wide enough to land aircraft," he said, laughing at the recollection.

Carson was such an influence on the young Arsenio that it was not by chance that he emulated the late-night star by becoming both a magician and a drummer, two Carson passions, and later, after becoming the host of his own nightly talk show, seriously considered launching his own line of men's fashions.

Aside from Johnny Carson, there was someone else who inspired young Arsenio—Cassius Clay, better known as Muhammad Ali. In fact, the first Rolls-Royce Arsenio Hall ever saw belonged to the cocky prizefighter whose mouth was fast as his fists, and almost as deadly to his opponents.

"I was infatuated with Ali as a kid because of his self-confidence," Arsenio confided. "That's the way I am. I hit them with that punch he hit Liston with, that one you never saw, that phantom punch. That's what I hit late night with. Nobody ever saw it, and nobody expected it.

"Right now," he said in 1989, shortly after his Paramount show had debuted, "I am at the point in my career that he was in after his first Liston fight, and I am going to be the Muhammad Ali of late-night talk."

Thus it's by design, rather than by accident, that

Arsenio reflects the outward self-confidence and verbal swagger of Muhammad Ali, delivering lines like: "I'm not the black man that America thinks, stereotypically, all black men are. I went to the same schools you did. I socialize with everyone from Jackie Collins to Eddie Murphy. I listen to the music of Reba McEntire, to Bobby Brown. I'm very special. I'm gifted. I was SENT here to do this. Now, that sounds weird, but the bottom line is I sat back and laughed because I planned this since I was twelve."

If Arsenio had a childhood love other than talk shows, it was basketball, a game he still plays and the reason why he is today such a locked-in fan of the Los Angeles Lakers and a compatriot of many of the team members, especially Magic Johnson, who has become one of his closest friends.

"I've been a basketball fanatic ever since I was in tenth grade," he explained. "At first I started playing 'cause I got into girls. I was a little chubby and it was a way for me to lose weight, but then," he added, "I really got caught up in it. Still am. I used to play one-on-one all summer with this friend of mine. But when we got to college, he had the edge and made the basketball team."

A self-professed "basketball fanatic," the 5'11" comic still spends time playing tough one-on-one, only for the last ten years he's been playing it at the Hollywood YMCA. "It's a nasty gym rat hole," he laughed. "These guys have been slamming me into the wall for years. Guys with teeth missing, with names like No-Neck. But it's where the material comes from. It's real life."

By the time Arsenio was twelve years old, he had already made his theatrical debut "as a piece of bacon in a sixth-grade play" and was entertaining at weddings and parties—a chubby youngster with a big grin who billed himself as "Arsenio the Magician." He also was working at Jean's Fun House, a magic store in a downtown arcade on East Ninth Street, doing card tricks.

A performance at a Cleveland Browns football party led to an appearance on a WJKW-TV show called "Rap" and later to his own WXEL-TV, Channel 8, television special, "The Magic of Christmas." "I finally learned how to pull a bird out of a hat," he would later say, adding, "and then the little thing got so excited it left a present on my cuff. But I got such a good laugh about it I used to put some paste on my sleeve and kept it in the act."

But his first love, as he announced to his mother one day, was talk shows. "I'm going to do what Johnny Carson does," he told her. And, like most mothers would, Annie Hall just smiled and shook her head, and sometimes wondered aloud about "where that boy gets his wild ideas."

But Arsenio believed. He had faith in his abilities. And he had hope for a better future. So he kept watching television, practicing his magic, and playing his drums—until his mother had to sell them one day when she discovered money was in short supply. A while later, though, when times were better, his mother bought him a walkie-talkie as something akin to a consolation prize.

Arsenio was in heaven. He used the walkie-talkie to interview the neighborhood kids, practicing, of course, for the talk show that he just knew was in his future. "Sometimes," Annie Hall recalled with a laugh, "I'd hear the other kids' parents yelling, 'You stop telling that Arsenio our business!'"

Arsenio was popular in high school, but he was

essentially a loner and didn't belong to any one clique. He did, however, have a best friend . . . at least for a while.

"Yeah, there was this guy who was my best friend in school," he once bitterly recalled, "and he tried to fuck my girlfriend. She called me one night and said, 'He has two tickets to see the Dramatics, and his girlfriend's busy. Is it okay if I go with him?'

"I said, 'Sure, go 'head.' So she went, and he grabbed her. And he was the best friend I ever had. It's been like that over and over again. Whenever I try to get close to someone, something like that happens. That's why," he would admit years later, "I find it difficult even today to trust anyone." And perhaps that's why, in later life, Arsenio would consistently "do unto others" before they could "do unto him."

Although Arsenio always knew that he wanted to be involved in show business, he rarely received any encouragement from his friends or family. Instead, he would later recall, he was constantly reminded that he was black, and would have phrases like "You have to pay for your color" tossed at him.

"There's no positive affirmation in the ghetto," he has repeatedly said. "All my life I was told that I couldn't do what I wanted to do. These days I'm constantly telling kids to believe in themselves. But when I was younger, I let people convince me that it was not possible.

"In my neighborhood," he continued, "it wasn't so much the white man as it was us allowing America to convince us that we didn't have it. It was a self-esteem problem that you suffered constantly by watching television and not seeing people who looked like you, from constantly being subjected to racism."

"I had relatives and friends telling me, 'It's all

right to dream, but it's a white man's world' when they should've been telling me, 'Fuck that, you can do anything you want.'

"The word 'nigger' was created by the white man as an oppressive term," he continued, "but in my neighborhood it was used all the time in reference to each other. It was taking this vicious slur and accepting oppression."

Throughout high school, Arsenio's relatives and various guidance counselors advised him to pursue a trade so that he could have job security after high school. If he was lucky, they repeatedly suggested, perhaps he'd get a job working at a factory. "Everyone always thought I'd end up working at Republic Steel or at the rubber plant in Akron," he would later laugh, but not without a slight trace of bitterness to his voice.

But Annie Hall was determined that her only son would go to college. In fact, she was as determined about that as Arsenio was that he was going to be an entertainer. Since they were both stubborn, Arsenio's future became a tug of war during his early high-school years.

Looking back, Arsenio cannot remember anything else that he and his mom ever fought about. But they did fight. And once, when Arsenio told her he didn't want a higher education, she slapped him across the face. "You're going to college, or you're moving out of this house," she angrily told him.

"You see, I figured I'm talented, I'll be an actor, I'll be a comedian," Arsenio later recalled. "Plus there were baaadd things on TV, like 'Good Times' with Jimmy Walker. Hell, I could've quit school in the sixth grade and played J.J.," he said with a chuckle.

In the end, of course, Annie Hall prevailed. "You're going to speak the English language like

Sidney Poitier," she told him. Then, convinced Arsenio was falling in with the wrong high-school crowd, she packed their belongings and moved to Warrensville, a racially mixed blue-collar suburb of small houses and a lot of apartment buildings, so that Arsenio could attend John F. Kennedy High, a more college-oriented school.

Once Arsenio was enrolled, Annie Hall went to the school and talked a guidance counselor into writing a letter of recommendation for her son, just in case his grades didn't measure up for college entrance.

Although his mother could not relate to his grandiose dreams, she did believe in Arsenio and was supportive of him. Whenever he began losing faith in himself, she would always intervene. "If you are going to let them discourage you, I don't want you," she'd tell him.

According to his mother's recollections, Arsenio was so introverted he never went to a party until he was sixteen-years old. Annie Hall thought it was because he was shy around girls. But the truth was, Arsenio would confess years later, that he was overweight and always too embarrassed to ask anybody to dance.

It was because of his weight problem, plus the fact that he had to wear special orthopedic shoes as a young child, that Arsenio turned to comedy to hide his insecurities and win the goodwill of his classmates. What better way to disarm a potential hurt or a possible enemy than through laughter? It is a lifelong pattern he still employs, off camera and on.

"When I'd get to school, I was a nut," he recalled with a laugh. "I was the classic class clown. I was the fat little boy. Short, too. I can remember in first grade trying to turn my eyelids upside down for the cute little girl, Vetrella, sitting next to me. These folks were like an audience, and I had them until 3:30 P.M. every day to do this show."

The minute one of his teachers would leave the classroom, he'd be up in front of the blackboard, imitating them. "I think I did have Miss McDonald down pretty pat," he would later recount, adding, "She spoke oh-such-perfect English, the Barbara Jordan of Charles Dickens Elementary School."

Then, after school, he'd continue his steady stream of jokes while practicing with the marching band in which he was the drummer. Music has always been a large part of Arsenio's life. At one point, he even had his own musical group.

While his classmates laughed at his antics, his teachers were less than receptive. Not only was he once suspended from school for calling a freckle-faced teacher "Cookie Man," the teachers made fun of his show-business ambitions. Everyone was aware his dad was a Baptist preacher, that an uncle was a bartender, and that another uncle worked in an auto body shop.

"I was always told to be like somebody else," he recalled. "My mom would always say, 'You should be like this person, you should be like that person.' She never said, 'You're great. Be like you.' Anytime I dreamed, I was shot down by people who called me crazy."

Despite the gibes and the potshots, however, Arsenio was undaunted. "I'm going to go to Los Angeles and I'm going to have a star on Hollywood Boulevard," was a constant refrain he'd tell people. And they'd say, "Where does he get this? What is wrong with him?"

But someone believed him.

The caption beneath his 1973 senior high school photo reads: "Talk Show-Tech."

CHAPTER

2

The first person in his family ever to attend an institution of higher learning, Arsenio wore the mantle of college student with a deep sigh of resignation. To him, school was nothing more than an obligation to his mother and a waste of four otherwise good years.

Nevertheless, he enrolled at Ohio University as a speech major, determined not to disappoint his mother, even though his heart, as always, was filled with a passion for show business. Thus, when a guidance counselor during his freshman year routinely asked him, "What do you want to do when you get out?" Arsenio replied without hesitation, "I want to go to Hollywood and be an entertainer. I'd like to have a talk show."

"Come on, Arsenio, wake up," the counselor had responded. "There are stars, and there are audiences. Some people have to accept that they're just going to be a part of the audience. And you're one of those people."

It was a cruel and insensitive response, and for anyone with less faith and determination than the future "A-Man," it would have been a devastating blow. But for Arsenio it merely served to strengthen his resolve. He was not going to be a spectator, watching other people strut their stuff on stage. No sir. He was going to be a star. And then everybody would be sorry they'd had so little belief in him. He would, he promised himself, show them!

"I got on the forensic team at Ohio University and was asked by the coach, Dr.[Raymond]Beatty, to enter the after-dinner speech event," he would recall with a laugh. "I wrote something about the cultural shock of being on your own in college and doing things like laundry. I got such a kick out of writing routines that I knew I just had to keep on writing."

After completing his sophomore year at Ohio University, Arsenio transferred to Kent State, and since his mother by that time had moved to Chicago, he lived for a while with his maternal grandmother, Elizabeth, who was ill. "She was my best friend back then," he would later recall. "We were like roommates. She taught me how to clean a .38 revolver, and she used to help me work out my problems with women."

By the end of his junior year, however, Arsenio was living off campus in a well-furnished one-bedroom apartment and was driving a late-model white Grand Prix, thanks to Annie Hall's well-paying job with the Teamsters Union. Not a bad life for a struggling college student. "It was his mother," explained Annie Brown, a fellow speech major at Kent State. "She gave him everything he wanted. He was an only child and I think she spoiled him 'cause his apartment certainly wasn't typical of a student."

Annie first met Arsenio when he sat next to her in a class in Engleman Hall and began copying her notes. Once they'd become friends, Arsenio nick-named her A.B. and one day confided to her, "I want to be a comedian." The class they shared was called Survey of Radio and TV; and it was a cinch for Arsenio, a lifelong TV addict.

"Yeah, the class was a piece of cake for Arsenio. He always was asking questions, making comments, even trying to outsmart the professor," Annie recalled. "So after a week I went up to him and asked him if all he did was watch television.'Yeah,' he told me. 'I love TV. I could teach this class.'"

Nevertheless, he still counted on Brown to take notes on the course, which she did for her own sake. "Arsenio used me to his advantage in class," Brown laughed. "He talked a lot while I took good notes, then later he copied MY notes. We studied together a lot, too, but studying with him was never easy," she added. "He was constantly making jokes—about me, class, life in general, people who would walk by my door.

"The night before our final exam, we studied together in Arsenio's apartment," she continued, and he fixed me several white Russians while we crammed. The next day I overslept for the 8:00 A.M. exam. Knowing that wasn't like me, Arsenio was worried, so he asked the professor if he could telephone me; but before he could do that, I walked in. Arsenio told me later, after class, that he felt guilty 'cause he was sure the drinks were the reason I had overslept."

Despite their studying, both of them got C's, instead of the A's they'd been expecting. Arsenio was depressed. "I can't believe it," he told Annie. "We studied so hard. We knew more than anybody else in that class." But according to Annie, Arsenio was never glum for long. "It wasn't his nature. He was too much of a clown," she explained. "He kept my friends and dorm mates in hysterics. But basically he was a loner, although he did have a girlfriend who was always tooling around campus in his Grand Prix."

While at Kent State, Arsenio had a show on the student radio station and, as a disc jockey, did dedications weeknights from midnight to 2:00 A.M. "We would call in our requests, usually ballads by Earth, Wind and Fire or the Commodores, and he would always play them," Brown recalled.

The fall quarter of his senior year, Arsenio landed the lead role in a student production of the musical *Purlie Victorious*. And, as Brown recalled, "His performance was splendid. He could sing AND act." Later, backstage, Arsenio was ecstatic as he told her, "A.B., this is me. I want to be a star."

It was while in college that Arsenio also had his first real brush with "the biz" when comedian Franklin Ajaye, who was traveling the college circuit, performing and plugging his seventies comedy film *Car Wash*, appeared in concert at Kent State.

"My mother still had to carry around all my magician's props when I performed," Arsenio would later say. "And here was this guy on stage just talking, with nothing but a glass of orange juice. I thought, 'Hey, I'm a communications major, I could do this.'"

After the show, Arsenio made it a point to go backstage at the student center and meet Ajaye. "He told me, 'There are a lot of people out there looking to make people famous, but very few with the talent to be famous. If you're really talented, you'll be successful and you'll make it. Just don't give up. It was just a few words, but what he said to me was very encouraging."

Annie Brown remembers Arsenio from that long-ago night because that was the first time she'd ever seen him. He was especially memorable for the suit he was wearing—a bold yellow, red, and brown plaid, which, as Brown laughingly recalled, made him look "like a clown." She had no way of knowing that Arsenio had dressed in his Johnny Carson finest for the occasion.

Arsenio graduated from Kent State in December 1977. Years later he would sadly recall how his father, Fred Hall, was not among the proud parents watching their children walk across the stage to receive their diplomas. "It hurt me real bad," he would confide. "No matter how close or unclose we were, he was my dad."

It's an interesting story because Arsenio never marched, clothed in cap and gown, through the graduation procession with his fellow students. Since it was midterm when he received his BA, there was no pomp and circumstance, no graduation ceremony until the following June. By that time, however, Arsenio had entered a sales training program with the Noxell Company, makers of Noxema products, and had moved to Detroit. Less than a year later Fred Hall was dead. He died on April Fools' Day, 1978, after suffering a stroke.

After less than a year in "Motor City," Arsenio decided there was more to life than worrying about marketing Noxema. He quit his job, determined finally to try his hand at stand-up comedy. "My girlfriend's brothers were in a musical group, and one night we went to hear them," he explained. "At the break something happened to an amplifier, so they asked me to go up and stall. I started telling jokes. That was the beginning of the end. Before I knew it, I'd given up my job and my dental plan. I was scared to death."

Years later Arsenio would explain that a book, *Risking* by Dr. David Viscott, had changed his life. "I'd always wanted to be a comic. Always. But I didn't have the balls to venture out and try because I was always afraid of failing. I had a good job in Detroit with Noxell. I was comfortable, except deep down inside I knew I was punking out.

"Then one day, after reading this book, I realized—it hit me like a bell going off—there is no person who's ever achieved anything for which he or she will be remembered without taking some kind of risk. Success is not safe."

Unhappy that her son, a college graduate, would quit a promising job with no steady employment in sight, Annie Hall told him, "Don't call me if you need money." And he didn't. Instead he moved in with her—at that point she had a top-paying job in the pension office of the Chicago Teamsters Union and a top-of-the-line condominium at the Pavilion complex, not far from O'Hare Airport.

Although Arsenio worked for a while as a Chicago department-store salesman, first selling cosmetics, then jewelry, his mother essentially supported him, as she had throughout college, while he took classes in improvisational theater and honed his comedy routine. "There were many disappointments," Arsenio has recalled. "I used to be out of work for long periods of time and suffered through a lot of stress. I took different odd jobs so I could pull my own weight." But he still wound up often having to borrow money from friends and relatives, wondering if he'd ever amount to anything.

During his two years in Chicago, Arsenio met a number of people, each of whom helped him to the best of their abilities. One of the first to fall under

Arsenio's spell was Ed Hellenbrand, who owned the Comedy Cottage in Rosemont, Illinois, which was less than a mile from Annie Hall's condo.

A tiny building at the back of a large parking lot, the Comedy Cottage was a small, dark, intimate club that seated only 110 people at its wooden tables so grooved by the carved initials of its patrons it was almost impossible to balance a drink on them. Yet it was the only club of its kind between the two coasts, and therefore was very big on the comedy circuit during the late seventies. George Carlin, Jay Leno, Rip Taylor, and Gabe Kaplan all worked there at one time or another.

"Everyone stopped in and did a little time," recalled Hellenbrand, who launched the club in 1975. "Some nights we'd be so packed, I'd have people sitting on the floor in front of the stage." By the time Arsenio found his way there in late 1977, the club was at its zenith.

According to Hellenbrand, he, not Nancy Wilson, as Arsenio has proclaimed, was the first person to "discover" Arsenio. "He wandered into the club one night, went up on stage, and I knew immediately that [he] was hot and going to be hotter. He came back every day that week." And within a short time, says Hellenbrand, he and Arsenio shook hands and agreed that "Big Ed" would manage him for 10 percent.

"I really got behind him," Hellenbrand said. "I started taking him out to dinners. We talked about the future and which way he should go with his comedy. At that time he was going in the direction of Orlando Reyes, who was Chicago's answer to Redd Foxx then, and too blue to book. I sat the two of them down and we talked until the sun came up about the best way to go, comedy-wise. And from then on, Arsenio didn't do any more blue humor."

At some point in late 1978 or early 1979, Hellenbrand went to Monroe Elfenbein, the manager of the Blue Max, an upscale nightclub at the Hyatt Regency Hotel near O'Hare Airport.

"I said to him, 'Look, finally I got two acts I think are capable of opening for some of your people. Will you come to the club and take a look?' He said, 'Sure.' He came over to the Comedy Cottage and I showed him Arsenio and Jerry Dye, a tall, thin hillbilly comic. And he liked both of them. He booked Arsenio as the opening act for Nancy Wilson and Jerry Dye with Jerry Lee Lewis."

Melba Caldwell, a Chicago agent who's been in business since 1961, also remembers Arsenio's early days in the Windy City and the first time she encountered him. "He called me and asked me to please come out to the Comedy Cottage to see him. But I told him he'd have to send me an audio tape of his act first. He did and I thought he was quite good. So I went out there and I remember I sat around and waited until midnight to see him and he was very cute, very clever.

"Well, we talked and he told me that he needed to get bookings for larger audiences," she continued. "I remember him even telling me he'd work for nothing. So, a while later, I managed to get him a job as the opening act for Nancy Wilson for a Kappa Alpha Psi convention at the Hilton Hotel. As far as I know, that was the first time Arsenio ever met Nancy Wilson. He did a wonderful job. So I introduced him to Sparky Tavares, Wilson's road manager, and I believe it was Sparky who got him to John Levy (Nancy Wilson's manager)."

Several years later, in 1982, when Wilson was

returning to Chicago to perform at an Urban League benefit, Melba thought it would be fun to have the two appear together again. So she called Hollywood and spoke to Roy Gerber, who was then Arsenio's manager, and hired him for to open for Wilson for $1,250.

"He came in, stayed about two days, and it took me almost three years to get my $125 commission," she laughed. "He was always telling me, 'If you do this for me, I'll never forget you.' I'm not saying I believed him," she added, with a chuckle, "but I gotta admit I didn't think he'd forget me that soon."

Like many others who've met Arsenio along his road to success, Caldwell found him to be "very aggressive, clean-cut, intelligent, and funny." "I never signed him up as a client," she said, "because in those days I still thought your word was your bond."

At the same time that Arsenio was spending time entertaining audiences at the Comedy Cottage, he was appearing at other clubs, like the Maroon Raccoon, the Comedy Womb, and Zanies, as well as doing concerts. He had even opened for Blood, Sweat and Tears, which he considered to be his first real gig, shortly before his path crossed Nancy Wilson's.

"Arsenio," said someone who knew him then, "was an aggressive self-promoter, very self-centered and not afraid to pound on doors. He worked all the rooms around Chicago and a lot of the comics—Bob McDonald, Larry Reeb, Ted Holum, Ed Fiala—knew him. But a lot of the comics are bitter because after he left Chicago and made it big, he never gave them any help, never put any of them on his show, not even once."

Determined to get as much exposure as possible, Arsenio spent many of his Sunday evenings performing at the weekly Sunday-night amateur competition put on by singer Jimmy Damon at the Chicago Playboy Club on East Walton Street. As one of the club's winners, Arsenio got to open for a regular Playboy entertainer at the Chicago club, as well as at the Lake Geneva, Wisconsin, club.

"Yeah, he used to be a regular at the Playboy Club amateur nights," Damon recalled. "He'd drop by even on nights he wasn't appearing just to watch and learn. We were pretty close in those days, but now . . . I've sent him letters over the years, but I never got anything in return, which makes me kinda heartbroken. I mean, you'd think somewhere along the line there'd be a mention, a something."

Whether Wilson first met Arsenio at the Blue Max or at the black fraternity convention, the fact is she was captivated by the young comic and reportedly told him, "You don't belong here. You belong in Hollywood." Arsenio couldn't have agreed with her more.

"Nancy Wilson told me that in the course of her career there had been three acts she had tried to help—Bill Cosby, Richard Pryor, and Arsenio," Hellenbrand recalled.

Twelve years later Wilson would recall that she was particularly struck by Arsenio's well-focused ambitions, as well as his ability to work the audience. "I thought he was very amusing," she explained, "and I wanted John [Levy] to see what he could do to help him.

"I wanted to make sure Arsenio had an opportunity because he was a very nice young man," she continued. "I thought he was a lot better than his material at that time, but his rapport with the audience was wonderful. The smile, and the fact that I could see he had a connection with the audience. He had them in the palm of his hand. I thought he had the ability to be really super.

"He knew what he wanted, and he knew who he was," she added. "Back then, who would have dreamed that Arsenio would get a national talk show. But it didn't surprise me one bit. I always thought he had that possibility."

Determined to help her ambitious young discovery, Wilson called her manager, John Levy, told him about Arsenio, and asked him to come to Chicago to meet Arsenio. "I flew to Chicago and met with Arsenio and his mother and we became like family," Levy recalled, adding he had heard about Arsenio from both Wilson and Tavares. As a result of the meeting he booked Arsenio to open for Wilson's November 23, 1979, Carnegie Hall concert.

Hellenbrand remembers it well. "I flew to New York and then, after the concert, Levy, Arsenio, and myself sat around discussing his future and what moves he should make."

As fate would have it, that was the last time Hellenbrand was ever in the company of Arsenio. "Wilson took him to the West Coast right after that," Hellenbrand explains, adding, "I didn't take a commission. I didn't think of it. But from that point on he didn't need me anymore and, well, I don't know any other way to put it, he shunned me.

"To this day, he's never answered my calls. He was a young fledgling comic when we met; but the minute he started getting some recognition, I guess you could say, he tended to believe his own press. Arsenio has a short memory," Hellenbrand concluded, offering an opinion many other people would share as they moved in and out of Arsenio's life.

The last time Annie Brown saw Arsenio in the

flesh was also in late 1979, when he returned to Cleveland as the opening act for Nancy Wilson and the Count Basie Orchestra in a benefit concert for the Kenneth W. Clement Center for Family Health at the city's venerable Palace Theater.

"He was nervous," she recalled, "but his routine was polished and clean. We talked after the show that night, and he said he would never be a 'blue comic' like Richard Pryor."

After her reunion with Arsenio, Brown became a major fan of her old college friend. "I helped him get exposure by writing viewer-response letters," she would later confide. "He would tell me who to write to and what to say. I would write the letters, sometimes two or three to the same person, and sign fake names. I made him look good, whether I'd seen him perform or not."

In May 1985, Arsenio appeared on "A.M. Cleveland," a local TV talk show. Hoping to reestablish their friendship, which had languished during the previous five years, Annie contacted the show's public-relations man and asked him to slip Arsenio a note with her telephone number so he could call her at work. But she's not sure he responded. "While I was at lunch, a man called, but he didn't leave his name," she said wistfully. Since then she's only seen her old college friend on television.

As for Arsenio, he rarely returns to Cleveland. On those infrequent occasions, however, he's found that "everything looks smaller. The sidewalks, the houses. It's all small. The only thing that still looks big is my daddy's old Cadillac," he laughed, adding, "Cleveland has been the great motivation for me to do well. I've always wanted to do good so I don't ever have to go back."

When Arsenio remembers those early days, it's with embarrassment, but not about the people he left behind. He's mortified by the quality of his stand-up routine, which, he readily admits, then consisted of lifting "things off a Richard Pryor album" and some "dumb things" he made up.

"It was amateurish. I'd talk about the Village People, like 'It's a mystery. You think these guys are gay?' And I'd imitate the Bee Gees, to show how singers don't enunciate anymore. It was terrible."

However, like "Big Ed" Hellenbrand, others who encountered the struggling young black comic in those earliest days had a different response. "Even then he seemed to have something extra," recalled Art Gore, a friend from Arsenio's early days in Chicago. "He had a rapport with the people; he could adjust his comedy to fit the audience in any club."

Once Arsenio finally found his way into the spotlight, he was addicted—caught up in the applause, the limelight, the acceptance of the audience. It was a magical elixir. He was determined and ambitious—two qualities that, if harnessed, usually add up to success.

More importantly, when he was in front of an audience, he was no longer that painfully shy, frightened little boy of his youth. "I see this confident, arrogant stage person and I don't understand how he gets it," Arsenio once confided, adding, "I do this magic thing in my head, and somehow I mentally become that guy."

Like many insecure performers, Arsenio learned during those lean days in Chicago that he was in control on stage. Forget the hecklers. He could handle them. He felt omnipotent. At long last he was safe.

And respected. And loved. It was an exuberant feeling to finally be somebody.

On New Year's Eve 1980, Arsenio made a momentous resolution. He decided he would leave Chicago and move to Los Angeles to lay his luck on the line as a stand-up comic. He was determined to either turn his dream into a reality or give up.

Having made up his mind to make the move, Arsenio wasted no time. Three days later, on January 3, 1980, he packed his few belongings into the smallest U-Haul available, crammed a beanbag chair and crate of albums into the backseat of his brown Ford Pinto, and headed west, driving almost nonstop from Chicago to Los Angeles.

Trying to conserve his meager savings, Arsenio spent his first couple of weeks in Los Angeles living in a shabby, roach-infested, eighteen-dollar-a-day Hollywood motel on Sunset Boulevard, where he went to sleep every night listening to pimps beating up their hookers.

He spent most of his days trying to land work as a comic, and often played basketball at the Hollywood YMCA, working off his frustrations at a career going nowhere fast and wondering if he had made the right decision.

"I always had a fear I was wrong for the business," he would confess years later. "I'd heard that most comics have unhappy childhoods. The comics I met when I got to Los Angeles had just gone to Freddie Prinze's funeral. They would always tell me, 'Remember, there's a fine line between comedy and tragedy.' And, of course, they were right.

"I watched my idols," he continued, "and I'd see the same thing. A lot of Richard Pryor's comedy came from pain; his mother was a prostitute and his grandmother was a madam. I'd hear Eddie talking about his father being an alcoholic.

"I didn't have that to draw from, you know. We were poor, but we were basically a happy family. 'Who wants to hear about us going to church?' I wondered. 'Am I less hungry? Maybe I won't make it.' Finally," he said, "I worked it out that you don't have to have a tragic life and be an unhappy, angry person to be a successful comic. You can find the humor to whatever you are."

Only weeks after arriving in Los Angeles, Arsenio moved into the Beverly Hills home of John Levy, where he remained for five or six months before renting his own apartment on Poinsettia Street, just south of Sunset Boulevard. By that time, thanks to the efforts of Wilson and Levy, his career had slowly begun to gain some momentum. "I was never really his manager," Levy recalled, adding "I don't know why, but comedy just isn't for me. I took him around, though, and introduced him to some people, like Mitzi Shore at the Comedy Club."

Levy also landed Arsenio his first real job in Los Angeles, which was as the opening act for one of his clients, singer Joe Williams, at the Parisian Room, a now-defunct black jazz club at Washington and La Brea. "Arsenio was a very nice person, a very easy-going person," Levy recalled, "but he got slaughtered that night. He just wasn't that good of a stand-up comic, at least not back then. But he knew what he wanted. He talked about having his own talk show even in those days."

As his self-appointed mentor, Nancy Wilson signed him to open for her at the Dorothy Chandler Pavilion in downtown Los Angeles, as well as a number of her concerts across the country, and helped him get established. As a result, unlike others from his past, Wilson and Levy still remain friends of Arsenio, and Wilson has appeared on his syndicated Paramount talk show. And although Levy sees him only rarely, Arsenio has never failed to send flowers to his wife on her birthday. "I'm quite a bit older than Arsenio," Levy said, "and so I think I've been like a father figure to him."

It was with Levy's blessing in early 1980 that Roy Gerber became Arsenio's first long-term manager. A well-known and respected Hollywood veteran, Gerber was managing Jack Jones, Diahann Carroll, Vic Damone, Shirley Jones, Peter Nero, and a number of lesser- known talents when his path crossed that of Arsenio's.

"Cynthia Gilbert, my associate, caught him at the Roxy one night—he was opening for Patrice Rushen, a keyboardist, and she was very taken with him," Gerber said, recalling the events leading up to his initial meeting with Arsenio.

According to Cynthia Gilbert, she had been so entranced watching and listening to Arsenio on stage at the Roxy she had immediately raced upstairs to find him after he'd finished his act. "He was in his dressing room and I went in and told him, 'You're the funniest guy I've ever seen,' and I handed him my card."

"Cynthia came into the office the next morning," Gerber continued, "and she was very excited. She said, 'We've got to check this guy out. If he doesn't have a manager, I think we should represent him.'"

So Gerber made some calls and discovered that Arsenio was working with John Levy, whom he immediately telephoned. "I didn't want to take a meeting with Arsenio if John was his manager," he explained, "so I called him right away. John and I talked a bit about Arsenio and John told me he had no problem with my representing him."

So, after talking to Levy, Gerber and Gilbert set up a meeting at their Sunset Boulevard office with Arsenio for the following day. At the end of the conference it was agreed upon that when Arsenio's contract with Levy expired in several months he would join Gerber's client roster. It was the beginning of a seven-year relationship.

"Roy used every friend he had, trying to help Arsenio get started," Gilbert confided. "We were constantly on the phone with Arsenio's agents at William Morris, trying to get things moving." But despite the efforts of the William Morris Agency, Arsenio's first booking after joining Gerber was as the opening act for Jack Jones, another of his clients, who was doing a concert at the University of Nebraska. It was one of the first of many concerts and Vegas acts Arsenio would do in the ensuing years.

"It was hard," Gerber recalled of those early days, "because nobody would do anything with him. They didn't think he was funny. And a lot of the time he wasn't. He just didn't have the material. The truth is that Arsenio is not the greatest stand-up comic in the business."

Nevertheless, by the mid-eighties, Arsenio had opened for a variety of big headliners, including Aretha Franklin, Lou Rawls, Natalie Cole, and Stevie Wonder.

Years later, after he'd become a major celebrity, Arsenio would admit that it was during the Stevie Wonder concert that he first realized how addicted he was to being on stage. "The first time I recognized the addiction was when I opened for Stevie Wonder at the Rose Bowl," he explained, adding, "When you hear seventy thousand people laugh, you realize you are a ham and you need it. My ego was so huge, you had to put my car in low to get me home. The laughter, the applause. There is nothing more gratifying in the world."

CHAPTER 3

To make ends meet during those first lean years in Los Angeles, Arsenio did everything from stand-up to commercial voice-overs. In fact, it was Arsenio's voice that first spoke for Winston Zedmore in the original cartoon version of the hit film comedy *Ghostbusters*.

Later he crisscrossed the country as the warm-up act for Tina Turner, Wayne Newton, Lynda Carter, Robert Goulet, Tom Jones, Patti LaBelle, even female impersonator Jim Bailey, whom he opened for at the Sands Hotel in Las Vegas. In 1991, like others from his past, Bailey also charged Arsenio with having a very short memory.

"Arsenio won't even return my manager's phone calls," Bailey complained, adding, "and I'm the one who gave him his big break. That was his first big chance—coming on between my Barbra Streisand and Judy Garland acts in Atlantic City. At the time," he continued, "he was very appreciative. After his part was done, he'd go into the audience and watch me. I acknowledged him every night and made him take a bow. He was grateful.

"Maybe it's because I wear a dress," Bailey said, referring to Arsenio's nonresponse to his telephone calls. "But if that's a problem for him now, it certainly wasn't when he was starting out."

"I was just a hustler, man. I did everything from stand-up to voice-overs. You name it, and I did it," Arsenio would later admit, recalling those early days. "I did everything from episodes of a "Twilight Zone" to comedy sketches on cable television and Tab and Levi's commercials to co-hosting the late-night "Movie Macabre" with Elvira, just to make ends meet, you know."

At one point, he was so desperate for money, he even played a weekend gig, opening for a Johnny "Guitar" Watson, at a Borscht Belt hotel in the Catskills for $100, plane fare, and free food.

"I was totally out of place. I was too young, and had no idea what the Catskills were about," he would later laugh. "I bombed like Hiroshima. So, after the show, I went into the coffee shop, ordered bacon, and I'm telling the waitress, 'I've had the worst show of my life' and I hear a heavy Yiddish accent saying, 'It coulda been vorse.' It was Jackie Mason and he was very nice to me, something I won't forget."

After he opened for Aretha Franklin, Arsenio's fortunes began improving, thanks in no small measure to his innate talent for cultivating friends in high places and marketing himself. It is a talent that served, and still serves, him well.

"I always kept in mind that they were the stars, and I was the foreplay," he would later explain, referring to the headliners for whom he opened. To this end, he would always try to tailor his act to their tastes and to announce their entrances. But nobody gave him any valuable advice until his first opening night while touring with Patti LaBelle, as a last-minute replacement for Nipsey Russell.

"I asked her what she thought she'd like me to open with," he recalled, "and she said, 'Honey, it's your show. I can't tell you what to do. You do want you want to do.'"

So Arsenio went out and did his regular act. After the show, he went back to Patti's dressing room and asked her what she'd thought of his opening act. "Well," she replied, "I think some of the things you said in the dressing room were funnier than what you said on stage."

Message received, Arsenio went out the second night of the tour and did on stage what he'd been doing backstage. As a result he received the first standing ovation of his career. He and LaBelle have been close friends ever since.

Despite his success on the road, however, the constant traveling and the never-ending string of hotel rooms were not the life-style Arsenio desired. "I absolutely hated it," he would later recall of his days of living out of a suitcase. "And if you don't enjoy it, there's no amount of money they can pay you. Man, I opened for Neil Sedaka, and I was in hell. You end up doing stuff like, 'My name is Arsenio. It's a very unique name for a black name. In Greek, it means LeRoy.' And the room goes crazy! It's a totally different kind of humor."

For all the good things that were coming his way, however, there were numerous setbacks, like the time he was sitting in Gerber's office and overhead an agent for a big white star yell over the speakerphone: "I'm not gonna take a nigger out on the road with my client."

Another time, when he was opening for Lynda Carter, he was on an escalator at Atlantic City's Trump

Plaza Hotel, when a woman grabbed him by the arm and said, "You're a comedian, right?" Before Arsenio could even nod, the woman's husband glanced over at him, then asked his wife, "What's with that nigger?"

"He's not a nigger," the wife angrily retorted. "He opened for Lynda Carter!"

"Once you hear stuff like that, everybody's guilty until proven innocent," Arsenio confided. "I've programmed myself to stop using that word 'friend,' except to my mother, my woman, and maybe my manager. That's about it."

No, traveling the countryside or escalators with insensitive, ugly people like that was not what Arsenio Hall envisioned for himself. What he really wanted, at least for a while, was to perform as a comic at one of the hip Los Angeles comedy spots— like the Comedy Store or the legendary Improv. But neither club owner would give him a break until Billy Crystal was unable to show up for a gig at the Improv one night. Out of desperation, Bud Friedman, the club's owner, offered the vacated spot to Arsenio.

"He brought me on, and I killed the audience," Arsenio would later brag. It was that appearance that opened the Hollywood gates for Arsenio because the audience, expecting to see Billy Crystal and Jay Leno, was filled with talent scouts and television bookers from "The Toni Tenille Show," "The Merv Griffin Show," *and* "the Tonight Show." What they saw instead, of course, was Arsenio. And they liked what they saw. Arsenio was *in*.

Well, sort of.

What followed was a parade of TV opportunities, most of them awful, all of them forgettable. He appeared on a few talk shows and several game shows, like the "Match Game," then signed a two-year "new talent" contract with ABC and was promptly tapped to star in the network's 1983 summer series "The Half-Hour Comedy Hour." A low budget six-week outing produced by Dick Clark and placed opposite NBC's hit series, "The A-Team," the show was quickly ripped to shreds in the Nielsens by the "Team" and disappeared without a trace before the summer had ended.

Even though the network deal had allowed him to buy a new car and pay off the loan on his mother's car, Arsenio was unhappy about having signed the ABC contract. "In some ways I think it's a mistake to be locked into one network," he told a friend. "Last summer, I had to turn down a role in "Streets of Fire," a Walter Hill film, and you don't ever want to turn down Walter Hill. And," he moaned, "I also had a shot at a semiregular role on "Cheers." That's a quality show, one I wanted to do."

When his ABC contract expired in June 1985, Arsenio did to the network what he had often done in the past: he departed and never looked back.

"I remember there was this guy at ABC telling me, 'It's time for a salt-and-pepper team to hit, and I don't think you can make it alone. So we're gonna audition a white guy for you.' They brought in guys like Wil Shriner and Thom Sharp and Tom Dreesen," he recalled, adding, "a lot of people named Tom, and they told me to pick a white guy! PICK A WHITE GUY! It sounds like a bad Chuck Barris game show.

"So I picked Thom Sharp. Me and this guy, we didn't know each other from Adam, and they wanted us to do a six-episode summer series. It failed miserably."

Years later, after he had made his mark, Arsenio would still recall his experience during the brief run of the ABC show. "If I ever fail again," he would tell listeners, "it will be based on my own sensibilities. I will never, ever, let any executive, any producer, tell me what to do again."

The following year, Arsenio appeared on the totally forgettable, equally short-lived ABC revival of "Love, American Style." At that point, 1984, he was writing new comedy material, taking comedy classes at the Vincent Chase Studios, and living in his nicely furnished but modest one-bedroom apartment on Poinsettia in Hollywood. For exercise he'd play basketball at the park across the street or at the Hollywood YMCA.

Like the walls of his Paramount office and his home today, the living-room walls of his small apartment were decorated with dozens of framed photographs of Arsenio standing beside Jayne Kennedy, Diahann Carroll, Richard Pryor, Lou Rawls, and Joan Collins. "I put them up there because they're my accomplishments—the people I've worked with. It's my own little hall of fame," he told a visitor.

Still searching for his big break, Arsenio continued appearing at various Los Angeles clubs while slowly making inroads with his TV appearances. It was while performing at Mitzi Shore's Comedy Store in Hollywood one night in late 1980 that Arsenio first met Eddie Murphy, who had just been signed to his first year of "Saturday Night Live."

Arsenio, who has spent entire weekends watching television, remembered the night of Murphy's network debut. "You ever watch football players on the sidelines when somebody scores?" he asked. "Well, that's what it was like. Yes, yes, yes! Eddie scored."

When Eddie Murphy wandered into the Comedy Store that night, however, Arsenio still hadn't scored. Despite the encouragement of his supporters, and the efforts of Gerber and Gilbert to jump-start his career, the harsh reality was that three years after having moved to Los Angeles in pursuit of his dream, Arsenio was still struggling, still searching for his proper place in the Hollywood sun.

"He was a natural," Mitzi Shore, owner of the Comedy Store, later recalled. "And he just got better and funnier. He's wide open in his comedy. He's vulnerable, which gives him a loving appeal to his audience."

Shore said she believed that Arsenio got away with so many racial jabs because of his "nonhostile manner." One night, however, his manner turned totally hostile when, tired of being heckled by one of the club's patrons, Arsenio jumped off the stage and attacked the man, who, he learned later that night, was an attorney. "Arsenio always had a bad temper," confided a friend who's known him since he first moved to L.A. "And he still does."

Concerned about a possible lawsuit, Arsenio telephoned Cynthia Gilbert the following day and had her write the man a letter of apology.

In 1984, shortly before his television career began to soar, Arsenio was taping a segment of "Hollywood Squares" at the NBC studios in Burbank. "During a break," he would later confess, "I went over to 'the Tonight Show' set, moved a few things, and sat down in Johnny's chair. It was dark and empty on the stage, but I just sat there, taking it all in."

It was a private moment of affirmation for Arsenio, who, returning to the game-show set, was convinced more than ever that his future, and his future fortune, rested in having his own television talk show. So, when he was offered the opportunity to be second banana on a new network gabfest not long afterward, he jumped at the chance.

Unfortunately the show turned out to be yet another short-lived calamity titled "Thicke of the Night." An ill-fated attempt by Metromedia to corner the late-night market, the talk show starred Alan Thicke, a popular Canadian radio and television personality who was essentially unknown in the States. Thicke had first encountered Arsenio in 1981 when he had appeared on his afternoon talk show. He found him to be funny, quick, and charming.

"If you stand in front of somebody and they're laughing, it's difficult for you not to at least smile. So," Thicke once explained, "when Arsenio stands in front of you with that face and that enthusiasm and that hand-in-a-cookie-jar kind of look, you're halfway there. I recognized that in him way back when, and just thought he had a good comedy attitude."

After going through a series of format changes on "Thicke of the Night," the producers finally hired Arsenio as the host's sidekick. Frank Stallone, singing brother of Sylvester, had already been signed on as the show's answer to Doc Severinsen. Despite the addition of Arsenio, however, the show was a disaster from its beginning to its premature end less than a season later.

"Being Alan Thicke's Ed McMahon—the statement is a nightmare," he would later laugh. "I used to get teased at the Comedy Store about that. It was like being the son of Manson or something. I was the announcer and would sit with him on the couch, and I felt like the halfback on the Indianapolis Colts.

"I used to sit there on that couch and think, 'I wish

they'd give me the show. This should be mine. I can make it work.' I remember the time we did a sketch and Alan didn't show up. So I got to do the top of the show. I was in heaven, man. I was in my world."

But the late-night talk show, like all others before it, failed to make even the slightest dent in NBC's "Tonight Show" ratings. It went off the air before most viewers even knew it was on. "It was a fiasco," Arsenio admits. "I was in hell again. But I was so hungry. . . . Things like that teach you not to do stuff just for money."

His brief stint on the Thicke show, however, also taught Arsenio a lot about what to do, and not do, on late-night television. As he explained, "This is no disrespect to Alan, but he tried to do everything. He was like Michael Jordan. He scored sixty points every night and never won. At 6:00 P.M., Alan would still be rewriting the show, and the taping was set to begin at 7:00 P.M."

As for Thicke, he has nothing but kind remembrances of the young comic. "I know writers who removed my name from their résumés," Thicke once joked, referring to the show's demise. "But Arsenio remained a friend in failure, and you learn to appreciate those people in a year like that.

"I've always respected the killer instinct in Arsenio," Thicke added. "It's an important element—the thing that transcends talent and makes it a business. There are great talents who don't have the business sense to go after the right liaisons and create and package themselves and their material. It takes a real cold, calculating business eye to know how to make the right moves with the right people and map out a career plan—and have the balls to go after that plan. And Arsenio does."

Arsenio followed "Thicke of the Night" with two

forgettable seasons (1985–86) on "Solid Gold," the longest-running syndicated music show in television history. Although Arsenio had opened for co-host Marilyn McCoo, the two really hadn't known each other well until they found themselves appearing together on the series.

"He definitely enjoyed himself, but the one thing that always concerned me was I thought Arsenio was funnier than the material they gave him to do," McCoo would confide six years later. "I was sorry they didn't give him a chance to do his own stuff. But he would come up with some marvelous ways of delivering the material to make it work.

"He always had a wonderfully engaging manner," she added, "and I think that's one of the reasons for his success. His likability factor has always been very high."

Even though he'd put on a happy face for McCoo and the crew, Arsenio would later admit he hated co-hosting the show. He found reading cue cards to be less than creative for a man of his talents, but he needed the money.

By the mid-eighties, though, things were beginning to happen. Granted they were small things, like a guest appearance on "Late Night with David Letterman," a writing credit on the Smokey Robinson special "Motown Revue," and, finally, a guest spot on "the Tonight Show"—on one of Carson's nights off from the show when Joan Rivers was the guest host.

"I would audition and audition for Carson," he would later recall, explaining he was always turned down. "They told me I was too green, too animated, too barbed. Sometimes they'd tell me I was too ethnic. Or I was too up. Or too physical."

Later Joan Rivers would recall listening to the

same criticisms about Arsenio from "the Tonight Show" producers. "He's barbed, he's this, he's that, put him on with me. That's the same stuff they'd say about me, too. But they wouldn't put him on," Rivers said.

According to a former "Tonight Show" staff member, however, the real reason Arsenio failed to get on "the Tonight Show" was that Johnny didn't like the way he looked. "He has too much gum," Carson reportedly said, referring to Arsenio's huge gums.

In fact, Arsenio's gums have been a constant joke between him and Eddie Murphy. "He jokes about my nose and my teeth being too small and is always telling me I'm fucking ugly," Murphy once laughed, "but he has huge gums and these long, fucked-up fingers. No, I'm infinitely better looking than Arsenio."

Then, one night in March 1986, just like in the movies, Arsenio finally got his big break when Patti Davis, daughter of then-president Ronald Reagan, canceled her "Tonight Show" appearance at the last minute. "Get Arsenio," Rivers told her manager, Bill Sameth.

"Yeah," Roy Gerber said, "I remember Bill Sameth calling about that. I went to Arsenio and told him they wanted him on the show and he asked, 'when?' 'Tonight,' I told him. And after all the times he'd tried to get on the show, he told me he didn't feel he was 'ready' and wasn't going to do it. I told him he was crazy. And, well, the bottom line is that he did the show."

That same year Arsenio had a chance to meet Bill Cosby backstage at the Sands Hotel when he was playing Atlantic City. "I'm going to tell you something," Cosby told the young comic between puffs on his cigar. "I don't know the secret to success, but

I do know the secret to failure. And that's trying to please other people.

"So," Cosby said, taking an extra large puff on his cigar, "Do what YOU want to do, Arsenio. There's only one Arsenio Hall on this planet. Please HIM. BE him."

In October 1986, Joan Rivers reportedly infuriated her supposed mentor, Johnny Carson, by taking over the reins of Fox Broadcasting's fledgling talk show, "the Late Show," without having the courtesy to tell him about the offer first. Carson was hurt. He apparently considered Rivers's action to be a slap in his face, since he had been one of her earliest and staunchest supporters.

However, what goes around comes around. As it quickly turned out, the "Late Show" was a personal, as well as a professional, disaster for Rivers. In rapid succession, the comedienne found herself failing in the ratings and then saw her husband, Edgar Rosenberg, who was also the executive producer of her show, barred from the set by Fox executives who believed his presence was too disruptive. When Rivers protested Rosenberg's dismissal, she was summarily dismissed on May, 14, 1987, less than nine months after having taken over the show on October 9, 1986.

Before she was dropped from the show, however, the comedienne had again come through for Arsenio, once more booking him as a last-minute guest, this time for an ailing Frank Zappa. It was a stroke of good fortune for Arsenio when, after Rivers's departure, he was offered another last-minute opportunity, only this one was big time.

When Suzanne Somers was canceled as one of the

twenty-seven different guests Fox had used to fill Rivers's vacated throne, the show's talent coordinator thought of Arsenio. She contacted Gerber to see if Arsenio would be available to host the show, not for a night but for the entire week. And, of course, Arsenio was available. He did the show, and by the end of the fifth night, it was apparent to everyone that he was a hit.

Gerber immediately began discussing a long-term deal with Fox, trying to up both the money and the weeks per month Arsenio would be helming the show. "At that point, all they were offering him was one week a month and for very little money. So I was in the middle of trying to negotiate a better deal," Gerber said, "when, suddenly, the woman I was negotiating with at Fox told me she couldn't continue working with me because Arsenio had a new manager.

"I remember being very, very surprised," Gerber said, "because I'd spoken to her on a Thursday afternoon and she told me this on the following Monday morning. I remember because I was flying out that same night to go on the road with Diahann [Carroll] and Vic [Damone]."

Like all of his predecessors, with the exception of John Levy, Gerber did not have a signed contract with Arsenio. " He and Arsenio shook hands, " Gerber said, adding, "Signed contracts are only as good as the people who sign them, anyway."

Unlike others who have watched Arsenio come and go from their lives, however, Gerber bears no ill feelings. "Look," he said, "we did a job and we were paid for that job. End of story. The only thing I find sort of amazing is that not long before this happened, I'd said to Arsenio, 'What would you like for your birthday?' And he'd said to me—and he was looking me in the eye when he said it, too—'The only thing I want, Roy, is for you to represent me one more year.'"

Unbeknownst to either Gerber or Cynthia Gilbert, Arsenio had agreed to sign a management contract with [Eddie Murphy's manager,] Bob Wachs, a former attorney and owner of New York's Comic Strip club.

Arsenio's explanation of his departure from Gerber, of course, was an entirely different tale, one he has told the press on numerous occasions. According to this version, his manager at the time had made it clear to him that he didn't want Arsenio to do the show. "The last thing he said to me before he went off on a cruise was 'You do her show, and you can find yourself another manager. Well," Arsenio would always add with a laugh, "Fox called me again and I did it—and I found myself another manager."

The real story about his relationship with Bob Wachs, and what actually occurred during those thirteen weeks Arsenio was taping the Fox show, would not emerge until 1990, when the two underwent a bitter breakup and wound up suing each other.

"It broke my heart when he left," Cynthia Gilbert said. "I mean we were like sister and brother. You have no idea of the time we spent together. I couldn't believe it. In a way, I still can't. It's taken me a long time to get over it. We were so close for so long.

"But he told me they [Wachs's company, X-Management] had offered him a million dollars to sign with them," she said. "I remember him telling me, 'I can buy my mother a house now.' Of course," she added ruefully, "I also remember him telling me, 'We're going to make it. I'm going to be the next Richard Pryor and you're gonna come with me.'"

With Wachs as his manager, Arsenio finally got an offer to host the show on an ongoing basis. "Rupert Murdoch called 1-800-CAUCASIAN and no one answered. So they had to give me a shot," Arsenio would later joke.

But, all laughing aside, he desperately wanted the $100,000 gig, which, he would later tell friends, "saved my life."

As much as he wanted the job, however, he also wanted Rivers's blessings. Playing it "politically correct" but not knowing what to expect, Arsenio telephoned the comedienne to discuss the Fox offer. To his surprise and delight, "She said, 'You do it, and you do it well. This is a break for you, and you have to take advantage of it.'"

It was good advice, and although their relationship has cooled in recent years after Rivers's reportedly unexplained last-minute cancellation of an appearance on his show, Arsenio claims to have not forgotten her generosity.

Eddie Murphy, who by then had become Arsenio's best friend, echoed Rivers's encouragement. "If they let you do that show one night, the show is yours," he told Arsenio. "You and me," Eddie told him, "see things differently. You see yourself one day maybe guest-hostin' for Johnny. I see you BEING a Johnny."

As it turned out, everyone was correct. Within weeks of taking over as host of "the Late Show," Arsenio was gathering an audience three times as large as that of his predecessors, including the irascible Ms. Rivers.

"I was just a fill-in for Frank Zappa that first time, so I winged it," Arsenio later explained. "Whatever I felt like doing, I did. I figured I'd probably never be back anyway, so why not? I had nothing to lose and everything to gain. When they left me alone, I realized what I was doing was producing myself. They did what had never been done; they gave this black kid from Cleveland a chance to do a show."

The audience, both at home and in the studio, loved his slick humor, such as when he suggested that Don King might have a white hairdresser with an ultra-Caucasian sense of humor. They loved his vulnerability, such as when he confided to feminist Gloria Steinem that she intimidated him because most of the girls he dated only communicated in phrases such as "take me shopping."

They loved his boyish enthusiasm when he played one-on-one basketball with Elliott Gould, and gathered around the piano with actress Emma Samms, Magic Johnson, and heavyweight champion Mike Tyson for a rousing rendition of "When the Saints Go Marching In." And they loved it when, upon being asked by author Jackie Collins if he had ever considered marriage, Arsenio looked into the eye of the camera and straight-facedly responded, "Yep, one time . . . when this girl called me up and told me she was pregnant."

Within weeks Arsenio had become the irrepressible, irreverent darling of late night talk. There was nothing, and no one, not even himself, who was safe from his brand of humor. He joked about the size of his rear end, his enthusiasm for discussing fashion with his black guests, even the fact that his white producer had asked him not to wear his diamond-stud earring. As Muhammad Ali would proclaim while a guest on one of Arsenio's last "the Late Show" outings, "Arsenio Hall, you having a ball!"

And, indeed, he was. "It was spontaneous, loose fun that turned into a party," he would later concede. "No matter where you were in America, you had a keyhole to the Hollywood stars talking casually and having a good time."

Arsenio was so successful at the helm of "the Late Show" that Fox, who had only hired him to fill in for the thirteen weeks it would take to launch the "The Wilton North Report," a comedy news show, tried desperately to re-sign him as the host of the soon-to-air show.

Arsenio allegedly turned them down flat, not once but three times. He was not interested in working with the company, even though Fox supposedly had upped the ante to a $2-million, three year contract. He was also smart enough to know that "The Wilton North Report" was going to be short-lived. Not long after its debut it sank without a trace.

"I did their show for thirteen weeks and Fox offered me nothing. They acted like they were doing me a favor," Arsenio explained. "Never once did an executive come to see me. In fact, I was at the Ivy restaurant in West Hollywood one night when I spotted Rupert Murdoch [owner of Fox and all its subsidiaries] waiting for his car.

"I introduced myself and he started fumbling through his pockets for a ticket. He thought I was with valet parking. I told him, 'No, Mr. Murdoch, I do your show,' and he mumbled, 'Nice to meet you.'

"I gave Fox all I had. I worked my butt off for them and they didn't appreciate it."

A year after Arsenio's departure, the Fox network, faced with a late-night void after "The Wilton North Report" and several other replacement shows had disappeared into the annals of TV history, found itself in the awkward position of offering its viewers a second glimpse of Arsenio's thirteen-week "Late

Show" segments through reruns, which they billed as "The Best of Arsenio Hall." It was a dubious triumph for the comic, who by then had become the millionaire star of his own Paramount talk show.

When Arsenio departed the Fox lot in 1987 after the last "Late Show" taping, he wanted nothing further to do with the studio. Without so much as a glance over his shoulder, Arsenio had signed an agreement with Fox prohibiting him from hosting another network talk show before January 1989. Having already signed a motion-picture contract with Paramount, Arsenio had both eyes on the future. And the future was a big-budget comedy, which, titled *Coming to America*, had been written by its star, Eddie Murphy, who by then had become Arsenio's best buddy.

"My goal is to be a success and never do TV again," Arsenio bluntly told the Cleveland Plaindealer, his hometown newspaper. Nevertheless, he did agree to host the 1988 MTV Video Music Awards the following September.

"It's like being invited to George Wallace's birthday party. I'm on a wave of change," he said, adding, "They've started to include rap music and black air personalities." He was referring to MTV's expansion that year to include more black performers. He had accepted the job even though MTV was then under fire from the black community for not including more African-American artists in the program.

Arsenio would remain the host of the MTV awards ceremony until 1992, when he was suddenly and unceremoniously replaced by Dana Carvey, who had become the comic flavor of the year, thanks to his impersonations of George Bush and Ross Perot on "Saturday Night Live," and his blockbuster movie *Wayne's World*.

Perhaps it was coincidence, but Arsenio was replaced *only* after Newsday criticized his 1991 MTV appearance as being too much on "the cutting edge" and accused him of veering toward homophobia and sexism and just plain tastelessness in the joke arena.

"Comics are not ready to fail, because it hurts so much," Arsenio once confessed. "You're alone, and they're not saying, 'We don't like your material.' They're saying, 'We don't like YOU.' And it hurts. The whole thing is approval.

"When you're a comedian, you're a very selfish performer," he had continued. "You're the writer, the director, the star. I watch the Lakers and their camaraderie, then look at Michael Jordan, Chicago Bulls, one of the baddest boys I've ever seen play, and I realize how important team play is. When you're a stand-up comedian, who do you give five to? You've got no one to pat on the butt."

But Arsenio did have someone to "pat on the butt" and to share his dreams and his humor with: Eddie Murphy, "Mr. Box Office" himself.

CHAPTER

4

If anything was ever preordained, it was that Eddie Murphy and Arsenio Hall would become friends. The two have a great deal in common. For instance, both suffered the emotional upheaval of their parents' separation when they were youngsters. And both were young men when their fathers died, although the death of Eddie's father, who was shot and killed by a girlfriend, had to be far more traumatic for Eddie than was the death of his father for Arsenio.

As children, both Eddie and Arsenio had longed for a career in show business and both were indifferent students who regarded school as "a never-ending party, a place to get laughs." And both admitted they had started doing comedy because they "needed the attention" as children.

Moreover, both would-be comics begrudgingly went to college only to please their mothers. Unlike Arsenio, however, Eddie dropped out after only a semester to take a chance as a regular on the second incarnation of "Saturday Night Live" in 1980. Additionally, both idolized comedian Richard Pryor and had "borrowed" Pryor's material when they were starting out as stand-up comics, even though their humor and style admittedly differs.

As Arsenio once so succinctly described the difference between him and Murphy: "Eddie's more of a sketch comic. He didn't make it as a brilliant stand-up. But I'm into observations. I can joke about anything."

Where the two differ vastly is that Eddie never wants to be alone while Arsenio is habitually reclusive and never really wants to be part of a crowd. According to Arsenio, although he's lived in Los Angeles for the last ten years, not more than ten people have ever been to his house.

"When your role model is Elvis," Arsenio once explained, referring to Eddie, whose childhood dream was to be the Elvis Presley of stand-up comedy, "you'll have your entourage, and you're going to be a lot more flamboyant. I'm a lot more introverted and low-key. My role models were much more conservative. I always wanted to dress like Johnny and be like Johnny."

Indeed, by 1989, Arsenio had become more of a fashion plate than his idol. He had become a trendsetter, known for his colorful leather jackets, finely tailored suits, and cutting-edge hip-hop attire. In 1989, Arsenio's clothes were mostly from Sami Dinar, the Beverly Hills clothier whose boutique had been named one of the best men's clothing stores in the nation by *M Magazine* that year. Dinar put Arsenio into Italian style suits, with broad shoulders and more fitted silhouettes, as well as the double-breasted suits the comic personally favors.

In 1990, Arsenio's wardrobe was so extensive that a rumor began wafting through the tabloids that the talk-show host had installed a motorized clothes finder, much like dry-cleaning stores utilize, in his closet. However, the truth is that Arsenio's clothes are recycled several times a year and then are donated to the Weingart Center Association, a Los Angeles–based organization that assists the poor and the homeless.

One night in late 1989 Arsenio was watching television and saw Elton John wearing what turned out to be a pair of Jean-Paul Gaultier sunglasses with springs on the side. He immediately decided to expand his fashion horizons. "I thought they were the coolest," Arsenio recalled. Then, after the taping of his first anniversary program, Luther Vandross, who had been a guest on the show, threw a party at his estate. Although Sly Stallone, Janet Jackson, and several other major stars attended the soiree, Arsenio spent most of the night talking to Elton John about his collection of unusual, and expensive sunglasses.

"At his suggestion I went to Optical Outlook and bought a pair," Arsenio said. "I wore them on the air one night, and this girl said, 'Oh, those are very sexy.' And I would put a possum in my pierced hole if an attractive woman told me she liked it. So I started collecting glasses and wearing them. It's a cosmetic touch." Two years later his annual bill for this "cosmetic touch" was a reported cool $40,000.

By 1991, Arsenio had an entirely different look— new, single-breasted colorful ensembles with African patterns and vests, designed by his wardrobe lady, Sandy Ampon, whom he had first met when she was a fashion consultant on "Solid Gold." "It insinuates an awareness of the motherland," he once explained with a laugh while discussing his colorful garb.

At that point he was intermingling the single- and double- breasted suits with funky, laid-back outfits, such as when Bruce Willis was a guest. For that occasion Arsenio wore a black rayon shirt, black pants, and Reeboks.

Later that year, when Sting appeared on the show, Arsenio wore the standard musician look of a black T-shirt and chinos, highlighted by a black jacket with spangled armbands. And when Warren Beatty dropped by wearing his Dick Tracy trademark yellow raincoat and dark fedora, Arsenio greeted him by wearing the identical outfit.

According to Arsenio, however, he rarely knows what he's going to wear more than fifteen minutes prior to the show. But Sandy Ampon does. As Arsenio's wardrobe supervisor, she chooses his clothes for the evening according to her mood. "He's really conservative and I'm the other extreme, real courageous and adventuresome," she explained, adding, "That's what makes it interesting. Our tastes complement each other.

"Arsenio can wear anything from bright reds and yellows to aqua, teal, and blue," she continued. "He's got excellent taste. He's a designer's dream, and a joy to work with because he's willing to try anything and everything." More often than not, however, Ampon's game plan depends upon who is on the guest lineup that night. "If we have a really extreme rock or rap group on the show," she explained, "I think Arsenio should be concerned about losing the mainstream audience. So I tend to pull back and give him a more conservative look."

In an effort to keep Arsenio well dressed, Ampon usually goes on weekly shopping sprees throughout Los Angeles. One of her favorite shops has been the trendy North Beach Leather Shop, where most of Arsenio's leather jackets and vests have been purchased.

Arsenio's splashy print ties, like the one he gave Bill Clinton the night the candidate joined the Posse for two saxophone solos, come from master tailor Joe Cotroneo, a Hollywood haberdasher, which is where the majority of Arsenio's suits are now custom-made.

"I trust her taste to such an extent I haven't gone shopping for myself since November 1988," Arsenio admitted. "At this point she even dresses me to go play basketball."

Despite his public persona as a hip fashion plate, however, Arsenio off-camera preference is for nondescript outfits, like sweats and sneakers, T-shirts, baseball caps, and baggy pants. And Ampon buys them, too.

"You'll never see me in a pair of leather pants outside of TV," Arsenio once explained, adding, "It's a big problem with girls. They expect me to dress like this guy, always having everything together. I hate to say it, but I'm a bum. I have fights with Eddie about my attire all the time."

Eddie, of course, is Eddie Murphy, known to be a snappy dresser both off and on camera.

Although Murphy is two years younger than Arsenio, by the time the two met in the Comedy Store in the early 1980s, he had already become a major Hollywood star, a fact the relatively late-blooming Arsenio attributes to his having stayed in college while Eddie dropped out. "Eddie was sneaking into comedy clubs when it was illegal for him to be in them," Arsenio explained. "I went to college to be a sports announcer and fell into this. My image of comics was retards until I saw Richard Pryor and other 'cool guys' who did stand-up."

In the wake of his double triumph in *48 Hours*

and *Trading Places,* Eddie had already signed a $15-million contract and had earned the nickname "Mr. Box-office" on the Paramount lot by the time he and Arsenio started hanging out together. He was famous at nineteen and a millionaire by the time he celebrated his twenty-second birthday.

In fact, by 1988, the year *Coming to America* was produced, Eddie Murphy's last three Paramount films—*Beverly Hills Cop I and II* and *The Golden Child*—had grossed an awesome $674 million in worldwide ticket sales, which Forbes magazine estimated at approximately $27 million in earnings, making him the nation's fifth wealthiest entertainer in 1987.

So what was it about Arsenio that Eddie liked?

"Arsenio makes you like him immediately," Murphy once explained when asked about the twosome's enduring friendship. "He's got a real ingratiating smile, a very quick mind, and he's a very straightforward brother. He's funny and we have a lot in common—like comedy and a lust for women. We started hanging out because I was a fan and now he's my best friend.

"A lot of people have never seen his real stand-up, only the two minutes of his act he does on some stupid comedy show," Murphy added. "But watch him for a half hour. He's a bad motherfucker, and he knows how to work a stage better than anyone I know, including me."

According to Murphy, the two first met through Keenen Ivory Wayans, a mutual friend, during the filming of *48 Hours.* Arsenio's recollection was that they first met at the Improv in West Hollywood. According to Arsenio, "Eddie's mom saw me on the tube and she told him, 'I thought I saw you, but it was some guy who looks like you or acted like you. His name was Arsenio Hall.'

"Well," Arsenio said, "that made him want to see me, too. So one night when he was out on the West Coast and had just signed to do *48 Hours*, he came in to see me at the Comedy Store. He came up afterward—I knew who he was from "Saturday Night Live"—and he said, 'You don't look like me.' I looked at him and laughed. 'Who said I did?' I asked. And then he said his mother did, and I guess he was kind of embarrassed because he said, 'Hey, let's hang out.' And we did, and we've been hanging out ever since."

Well, not exactly. According to a friend who knew both Keenen Wayans and Arsenio then, Arsenio didn't like Eddie upon first meeting him. "I think maybe it was jealousy, but Arsenio was definitely not gung-ho Eddie in the beginning. It took a while, but then they really became tight, really good friends."

"We share intimate secrets," Arsenio has said of Eddie. "We cry together. There's no competitiveness between us. When I called and told him I had been signed by Paramount, he couldn't have been happier. Eddie," Arsenio concluded, "is like my brother, the brother I always wanted but never had."

Thus *Coming to America* was a dream come true for Arsenio, who, although he had appeared in an earlier film, considered this movie role to be his official film debut. In truth, Arsenio was so excited about the film it was all he could think about or talk about for weeks. As he confided to friends, every time he thought about the movie, chills of excitement would run up his spine. He could envision the nation's theater marquees ablaze in lights: "EDDIE AND ARSENIO! Together for the very first time ON SCREEN!"

Coming to America was on a wholly different scale than Arsenio's first movie, *Amazon Women on the Moon*, a 1986 collection of loosely knit vignettes, also featuring Rosanna Arquette, Carrie Fisher, and Ed Begley, Jr., that had been produced on a shoestring budget by Robert K. Weiss of *Kentucky Fried Movie* fame.

An Eddie Murphy film meant big budget, big studio, and guaranteed big box office. More important, the script offered Arsenio an opportunity to exhibit his range of comedic abilities. In addition to playing Semmi, the loyal friend of Prince Akeem, played by Eddie, he also called upon to portray a number of other characters, including a fiery preacher named the Reverend Brown and an elderly barber named Morris.

In short it was, in Arsenio's eyes, the chance of an acting lifetime.

The intricate makeup process to turn the two players into the film's various characters was an arduous task that had begun months before the movie even went into production. To do the special makeovers successfully, Rich Baker, the film's Academy Award-winning makeup artist, had to create casts of Eddie and Arsenio's faces. These were then used to make clay facial sculptures onto which Baker could sculpt foam rubber appliances. The hair, eyebrows, and mustaches of the characters also were specially designed hairpieces, with each hair hand-woven into a separate lace.

It was a time-consuming experience, which called for Eddie and Arsenio to spend hours sitting immobile in their makeup chairs, having the appliances glued and fitted to their faces. "Rick Baker sat down with us," Arsenio explained, "and looked at us and studied us, and took pictures. He said, 'Now, Arsenio, you have a huge smile and tiny ears. These are the things we're going to work on the most.' So as the barber, I got a different nose and different teeth and a beard, which took about two hours.

"But it took them four hours doing the preacher on me," he continued, adding, "Every part of my face was different. But I liked being Reverend Brown because it gave me a chance to use all the things I'd observed my father doing.

"I'll tell you," he laughed, "my daddy could cry on command, just like Jimmy Swaggart."

Like Arsenio, Eddie had worked with John Landis, whom comedian Chevy Chase once described as "an attack dog on a leash." They had made *Trading Places* together and had gotten along smoothly. This time out, however, there was tension between the two from the beginning. And nothing is guaranteed to divide a set and make life more miserable for everyone involved than a feud between the director and the star.

"When Eddie and I were writing the script [on a tape recorder in New York City's Mayflower Hotel], Eddie wondered who should direct," Arsenio would later recall. "I said, 'Well, I had a lot of fun working with John.' And Eddie said the most fun he had making a movie was with John on *Trading Places*. But when Eddie made that film, he was a young boy. When he came to make this movie, he was the number-one box-office star, only John didn't treat him any differently," Arsenio said, explaining the difficulties between Landis and Murphy.

Since Arsenio had worked before with Landis in *Amazon Women on the Moon* and was best friends with Murphy, the making of *Coming to America* should have been a highlight of his career. But it wasn't. *Coming to America* was a troubled film from its beginning to beyond its release. Within days after the start of production, it became apparent that life on the set was going to be stressful.

Arsenio, who was friendly with both Murphy and Landis, suddenly found himself in the unenviable, and certainly uncomfortable, position of trying to stay out of the middle of a quickly escalating conflict.

"I thought making movies would be a great change of pace," Arsenio would later admit, "but I found out that I hate to do movies. It was a nightmare. Making movies is very complicated, tedious, and tiresome. It is especially terrible for a comic, because you do a joke and you turn to people and ask, 'Was it funny?' They say, 'We'll let you know in eight months.'"

The tension on the set, in fact, was so great that Arsenio reverted to his childhood tendency of sleepwalking, as Annie Hall discovered when she arrived for a visit. "I was in bed, and he came walking into my room, saying, 'Mommy, Mommy.' I said, 'Arsenio, sit down.' When he woke up, he said,'How did I get here?' 'You walked,' I told him."

Although he kept quiet on the subject of Landis during the filming of *Coming to America*, Arsenio finally confessed in a 1991 interview that he "probably wouldn't work with Landis again." "I just did my job, because I was happy to be in the business. But Landis wasn't a nice person sometimes," he explained. "It was a great experience, but morally, I have to work with someone I truly like and respect."

Eddie Murphy would later attribute the deterioration of his friendship with Landis to the fact that he had not appeared in court in support of the director during his highly publicized Los Angeles trial for manslaughter in the deaths of actor Vic

Morrow and two Vietnamese children during the filming of *Twilight Zone—The Movie*.

Even though Landis was aquitted, when Eddie called and asked Landis to direct *Coming to America*, Landis's first words to Murphy supposedly had been "Where were you? They almost sent me to jail!"

The real core of the problem between Landis and Murphy, however, appears to have been their overly inflated egos. According to Murphy, shortly before the film was set to begin, Landis told him, "Everybody is afraid of you, Eddie, but I'm not. I'll tell you, 'Fuck you.'"

Why the two would continue to work together after this conversation remains a mystery, but the relationship did not improve as filming continued. If anything, it deteriorated, ending in an actual physical confrontation when, according to several crew members who were present at the time, the costume designer, Deborah Nadoolman, who also happens to be Mrs. John Landis, reportedly complained in racial terms about Murphy having kept her waiting for a fitting for more than hour.

Upon hearing this, Murphy grabbed Landis from behind with an armlock, turned to one of his buddies, and asked, "What happens to a guy who is not afraid of me?"

"They get fucked," the friend replied.

What happened next, according to Murphy, who, for months afterward loved to regale listeners with the story, was that Landis "reached down and tried to grab my private parts, but I cut his wind off. And he realized I was serious. He started crying and said, 'Eddie,' and ran off the set."

Two years later, in February 1989, Murphy still remained estranged from Landis, who, he said during an appearance on Arsenio's show, "has a better chance of working again with Vic Morrow than he does with me."

(By the end of 1992, however, all was apparently forgiven. It was announced by Paramount that Eddie would be re-teaming with John Landis and together the two would produce Beverly Hills Cop III sometime in 1993. The fact that Murphy's two previous films—*Boomerang* and *The Distinguished Gentlemen*—had not been box office hits probably contributed to Murphy's burst of forgiveness.)

Not all of Eddie and Arsenio's misadventures that year were limited to the set of *Coming to America*. The twosome also had a harrowing pre–Rodney King experience with the Los Angeles Police Department.

As Arsenio would later recall, he and Eddie were traveling down Sunset Boulevard late one night when two patrolmen pulled over Eddie's late-model white Corvette because, as it turned out, the license plates were expired. "They put us through all this humiliating stuff. The cop just gave us total shit," Arsenio angrily recalled. "Eddie tried to tell him that his people had taken care of everything. And the cop said, 'Your people aren't here. You're here.'

"He was incredibly mean and rude until these girls came up and stared at us," Arsenio recalled. "They started oohing and aahing, and finally the cop figured we must be somebody important. He went back to the patrol car, got on the radio, and then came back and apologized, telling us, 'Oh, uh, actually your plates are okay. You've got an extension.'

"And then he asks Eddie for an autograph for his kid! I whispered to Eddie, 'Don't sign shit!' But remember—I whispered. And then I signed, too. You sign the autograph, you stay out of the choke hold."

In 1988, Arsenio was not yet the pop icon he was to become after the birth of his talk show the following year. During the making of *Coming to America*, he was simply a funny young man with a potentially bright future. He was in awe of his star-studded surroundings, and a well-liked sidekick to Eddie Murphy, superstar. And glad to be just that, at least for the moment.

"Why should I mind?" he replied, when asked about playing second banana to Murphy, shortly before *Coming to America* was released in the summer of 1988. "Hey, when you're playing second banana to the number-one star on the planet, it's not a bad place to start. So, no, I don't mind being a co-star. What I want to know is, 'Was I good in the film?' I want to be good more than I want to be popular, which is why Eddie and I get along so well.

"Eddie," he continued, "is the only person I'm close to. "And when he isn't around, I don't mind being by myself. I go to movies alone. I go to a lot of places alone. Some people probably think I'm a party man, but mostly I stay home on weekends."

Despite his oft-stated preference for staying home, however, Arsenio has always been a hearty partier, a man about town, who, with Eddie Murphy by his side, would stay up most of the night, either bar hopping or partying at Eddie's place. Carlos and Charlie's, Nick's Fishmarket, and more recently Nicky Blair's and the Roxbury Club have all been favorite Sunset Strip hangouts of Arsenio's since the mid-eighties. They are all late-night restaurants and clubs close to Mitzi Shore's Comedy Store, another favorite haunt.

In 1987, for instance, during an interview he complained about having a hangover, not having arrived back at his West Hollywood condo until 7:15 A.M., and having to fortify himself with a Bloody Mary after a night on the town with his pal Eddie. By that time he'd removed the large photograph of his bare-breasted buxom blond former girlfriend, which had added an erotic touch to the decor of his bachelor lair.

"Arsenio was very sexual then and he's very sexual now," confided a former Hall intimate, adding that the comic was rarely without a girlfriend and often dated more than one person at the same time, usually women younger than himself and, more often than not, Caucasian women.

"It was always interesting to me," the friend admitted, "that the white women he dated were always sort of trashy and dressed like whores, while the black women were usually pretty classy. I know that must mean something, psychologically speaking, but I don't know what."

It's also interesting to note that although he has been spotted dining at Spago's with everyone from Paula Abdul to Emma Samms, over the last four years, Arsenio has steadfastly stuck to his story of being a reclusive homebody. "I get to my Laker games, and I go to dinner. But I'm not a premiere guy. I don't go to Spago. If you go to Spago, you're going to get attention," he has consistently said.

He did admit to going out late at night to grocery-shop, however. It was, he said, his way of keeping a foot in the real world and getting material for jokes. "Sometimes," he explained, "you want to go and walk around, hear people responding, hear what people have to say."

When his number-one party pal, Eddie Murphy, slowed down the pace of his social life two years ago, Arsenio soon could be found partying at least once a week with Magic Johnson at the Roxbury Club, a trendy Sunset Boulevard club, surrounded by his bodyguards and a bevy of beautiful women in a booth upstairs in the private VIP room. Sometimes Eddie was there, sometimes he wasn't.

"A guy asked me not long ago, 'How does Eddie feel now that his second banana has shed his skin and Eddie is slipping on it?' Arsenio said after his talk show had earned him his own superstardom while Murphy's films had begun to bomb at the box office. "I said, 'Eddie will never slip on any banana because I'll always be there to hold him, and he will always be there to hold me.'"

Thus, with Christmas 1989 only seventeen days away, Arsenio found himself climbing the steps of the Los Angeles County Superior Court on his way to defend the creative powers, and the honor, of his pal Eddie, who had found himself in the middle of a landmark lawsuit over the rights to *Coming to America*.

Claiming the film was actually based on an eight-page movie treatment, *King for a Day*, he had submitted to Paramount in March 1983, columnist Art Buchwald had filed a breach-of-contract suit on November 21, 1988, against Paramount Studios, seeking more than $5 million in damages plus a percentage of the film's grosses, which then totaled $128 million domestically.

Arsenio's December 18, 1989, presence in the courtroom created a sensation. Two guards were posted at the door, and before the session began several female sheriff's deputies had themselves photographed with him with a pocket camera one of them just happened to have handy. Other staffers asked the comedian for his autograph, then disappeared, their squeals of delight echoing through the doors at the back of the courtroom, after he obliged. It was bedlam until the bailiff yelled, "All rise!"

Taking the stand, Arsenio looked around, much like a kid in a toy store. "This is all very exciting," he said suddenly, explaining to the packed courtroom, "I do a talk show, but this is all very exciting."

Once on the stand, Arsenio testified under oath that *Coming to America* differed from Buchwald's story both in its overall concept and in its details. Murphy's idea, he explained, had been to create "a black fairy tale" in which Murphy was to appear "very gracious, very strong, very intelligent. We were going for all the wonderful qualities that a woman dreams of in a man and that a man wants to be."

In the early eighties, he explained, he and Eddie had discussed the idea of making a movie that would "portray a positive image of royalty in Africa."

"I was basically listening," Arsenio explained. "We were having a discussion about the fact that Africans in general have almost always been betrayed by this town. For instance," he explained, "as a kid growing up in Cleveland, I never knew there were skyscrapers in Africa. . . . This may sound funny, but I only knew about the guys who helped Tarzan and people who were on hunting expeditions. And they were all natives. I never knew about the riches and the wealth and the dignity."

According to Arsenio, Eddie had drawn on his own experiences in portraying the multiple roles in the film. For example, he said, Murphy's characterization of an old white man was based on director John Landis's father-in-law.

However, under cross examination from Buchwald's attorney, Arsenio was pressed about statements in his original deposition that differed from his recollections while on the witness stand, regarding the genesis of the Murphy script.

For instance, asked if he had seen anything written by Murphy prior to the pitch meeting with then-studio head Ned Tannen, Arsenio said he had noticed a legal pad lying around and guessed that perhaps the conversations he and Eddie had about *The Quest* had been scribbled down shortly before the meeting.

Pushed by Buchwald's attorney, however, Arsenio admitted that he had never actually seen anything Murphy had written until they had pitched Tannen on the film during the summer of 1987.

Arsenio's best defense of his surrogate brother, however, came when he has questioned about Eddie's ego. Hall's response was to tell the attentive courtroom audience how generous his friend had been in giving screenwriting credit to David Sheffield and Barry Blaustein, his two former "Saturday Night Live" writers, who had transformed his idea into the *Coming to America* script; and how the film *I'm Gonna Get you, Sucka!* had come from an Eddie Murphy idea for which Eddie had never sought any credit.

"Nobody will ever know that it came from Eddie's idea. The man doesn't have the ego that people might think he has, and he obviously doesn't need the money. He's a very generous man," Arsenio concluded, choosing not to mention that Eddie's name had appeared in the credits of *Coming to America* numerous times, despite his magnanimity in giving credit to Sheffield and Blaustein.

Arsenio was not asked to explain that even though he had also given up his screenwriting credit to Blaustein and Sheffield—"These writers could use the money they could make by sharing the writers' credit alone," Arsenio recalled Landis telling him. "They both have kids and all that kind of stuff."— Arsenio had still received $30,000 for his contribution to the controversial script via his contract with Paramount.

Later, outside the court, Arsenio angrily told the gang of reporters following him down five flights of stairs on the way to his waiting limo: "It's very unfair, what's going on. I'd rather loan Art Buchwald some money than go through this. I'm offended because Eddie Murphy is a very bright man. I'm a bright guy, and very talented, if I do have to say so myself. Why do we have to seek a stolen concept? It's insulting."

A year later Arsenio said, "Nobody knows what was in Eddie Murphy's heart other than me. The lawsuit was against Paramount and the press misrepresented the suit as being Eddie Murphy versus Art Buchwald, which it wasn't.

"Eddie never went to court. Eddie never appeared on the stand," he continued. "I went to court because Paramount asked me to. It wasn't for him or against him. I went in because I felt as a member of this family, I owed them. Plus, to cut all the bullshit, a subpoena will make you get real loyal to your family."

Arsenio was telling the truth. He had been subpoenaed and Eddie Murphy never did actually appear in court. However, Murphy was deposed by Buchwald's attorneys and stated in the deposition that Eddie had received the inspiration for the *The Quest*, the working title of his film treatment, while suffering from a broken heart following his breakup with girlfriend Lisa Figueroa, a beautiful Long Island, New York, biology student and sometime model, he had been steadily dating until 1986.

Two years later Arsenio explained how Eddie's heart had, indeed, been shattered by Lisa, who, according to Hall, had been "the one person he really loved."

"This girl was an angel when he met her," Arsenio explained, adding, "but I saw her change under the pressure. She began to think she was Eddie and, well, not too many people get to him emotionally and romantically, so he was messed up when they broke up. He was very hurt, very down during that time."

According to Murphy, it had been his "broken heart" that had guided him into structuring a plot about an African prince, so rich and powerful he could never be absolutely certain whether a woman loved him for himself or for his money. He had, he claimed, originally sketched out the idea on the back of his cousin Ray Murphy, Jr.'s, notebook riding in the back of his bus while during his Pieces of My Mind tour.

It was only after the trial that it was discovered that Murphy, despite his broken heart, had taken several of the many heartrending messages Lisa Figueroa had left on his answering machine, spliced them together, and recorded a greeting for callers of her sobbing pleas of "Please, Eddie! Please! I love you, Eddie! Take me back!"

The message was certainly not the average way of recuperating from a broken heart. But then neither Eddie Murphy nor his sidekick Arsenio could ever be accused of being average.

CHAPTER 5

In the late 1950s, Frank Sinatra was dubbed "Chairman of the Board" of a tight group of his cronies—Sammy Davis, Jr., Peter Lawford, Joey Bishop, Dean Martin, and for a while, Shirley MacLaine—which the press quickly nicknamed the Rat Pack.

Thirty years later, in the early 1980s, Rob Lowe, Emilio Estevez, Kiefer Sutherland, Demi Moore, and a handful of other young actors noted for their exploits off as well as on the screen, were nicknamed the Brat Pack by the media.

In the late 1980s, Eddie Murphy found himself heading up a group of young, talented black entertainers and, in a moment of marketing genius, deemed his following to be the Black Pack.

"We have a group I like to call the Black Pack," Murphy explained during a 1988 press conference promoting his new film, *Beverly Hills Cop II.* "We basically hang out together, and bounce ideas off each other." Ironically it was a phrase that would linger more in the public's mind than the movie he was touting.

At the time the Black Pack to which Murphy was referring consisted of himself, Arsenio, Paul Mooney, who had been Richard Pryor's chief comedy writer for fifteen years, Robert Townsend, who, only the year before had produced the hit black comedy *Hollywood Shuffle*, and Keenen Ivory Wayans, who was just then coming into his own as a comedy writer and comic after a brief stab at being a serious actor.

What these men had in common was that they had each begun their careers as stand-up comics, and had hauled their belongings to Los Angeles from various parts of the country in search of their self-proclaimed rightful place in the sun. And each of them had either worked for or become a friend of Eddie Murphy since arriving in the Hollywood environs.

Actually the Black Pack had been born out of jealousy and resentment over Eddie's overwhelming success in an industry offering few opportunities to black entertainers, and a conversation that Arsenio and Eddie first had while driving through New Jersey in Eddie's white Corvette in mid-1987.

"We were talking about making *Coming to America* and we said, do we go with Spike Lee or a no-name director we can control, or do we get John Hughes to do something with a black person? That's when we came up with the concept of the Black Pack," Arsenio later recalled.

"We always noticed that in the Brat Pack films, there was never a black person. The only black person was in a Tom Cruise film and played a transvestite. I don't know why John Hughes never had a black person in *St. Elmo's Fire*," he laughingly added. "At least you could have a black person start the fire."

Thus it was at Eddie's hotel room in the fashionable L'Ermitage later that year that Arsenio, Paul Mooney,

Keenen, a bunch of Eddie's underlings, and the usual following of Eddie's female admirers found themselves involved in an intense conversation about Eddie's "star" qualifications.

Someone, no one could remember who, suggested that given the same break on "Saturday Night Live," any one of them could have become a success like Eddie, who, not surprising, took offense.

As Arsenio would later recall, Eddie said, "You know I hate that attitude. You motherfuckers think I'm not talented and anybody can do this. Does being good have anything to do with this? That pisses me off. That was my shot and I did with it what a lot of people couldn't do," he said, pointing out that Garrett Morris had not gone on to greatness from *SNL* and that fellow Black Packer Robert Townsend had auditioned for, but failed to land, a *SNL* slot.

At that point, according to Arsenio's recollection, he took over the conversation, saying, "If we would stop raggin' on each other, talking about who's best and who ain't shit, then maybe we could come together. Why should we bicker when we could chisel a whole lot harder at success through unity?"

"Yeah," someone said. "Nobody's gonna cast us in a John Hughes film."

"Right," echoed someone else. "They got the Brat Pack. And we're the Black Pack."

A year later, shortly after co-starring in *Coming to America*, Arsenio had joked that "Eddie and I made our own movie because white America won't let us be in the Brat Pack. So, instead of being mad because we can't get a job at your store, we opened a store."

And in doing so, the twosome realized the power in managing their own productions. "It's not black or white," Arsenio had explained. "It's green and it's called m-o-n-e-y. Money.

"For so many years black performers participated as talent and died broke. Many of our great black stars died broke. That's why," he concluded, "I have insisted on being the executive producer of my own show. I'm not just talent on salary. I'm a stockholder and executive producer."

And so, at the end of 1988, they had all flown to New Jersey, where Eddie owns a gate-guarded mansion called Bubble Hill in Englewood Cliffs, to celebrate New Year's Eve, 1988, along with a few hundred other Murphy pals, including Janet and LaToya Jackson, Vanessa Williams, and Sugar Ray Leonard.

Raising a glass of bubbly, filmmaker Robert Townsend had proposed a toast only minutes into 1989. "Brothers," he had shouted above the din, "let the good times roll!"

And roll they did.

Townsend and Wayans, who had made their mark with *Hollywood Shuffle*, an acclaimed low-budget comedy based on the frustration blacks had found working against Hollywood stereotypes, collaborated on a second film, *The Five Heartbeats*, released in 1991, then went their separate ways.

Wayans produced and directed as well as starred in *I'm Gonna Git You Sucka!*, another low-budget 1989 box office hit parodying the seventies' flurry of black exploitation films, like the Richard Roundtree series of *Shaft* movies. The following year he put his energies into developing the satirical Fox Broadcasting Network series "In Living Color," which turned out to be a ratings hit.

While Wayans has been busily starring, writing,

producing, and directing "In Living Color," Townsend continued to focus his energies on films. He purchased a 16,000-square-foot building in Hollywood in early 1991 and turned it into a mini-studio, which he dubbed Tinsel Town-Send Studios, and wrote, produced, and directed *The Meteor Man*, a 1992 fable about an inner-city schoolteacher given an extraordinary gift after being exposed by a meteor shower.

And Arsenio, of course, took over the reins of a late-night talk show bearing his name and by early 1989 was comfortably ensconced in the lap of luxury at Paramount Studios. But even prior to that, while hosting the Fox "Late Show," he had quickly turned the Fox studio on Sunset Boulevard into something akin to a Black Pack clubhouse, with various members of the group hanging out in the dressing room, sitting in the audience, doing surprise walk-ons and occasional stand-up comedy on the show.

The night Eddie dropped in, for instance, the "Late Show" ratings rocketed, giving Arsenio a star status no one else had enjoyed at the helm of the Fox talk show. Eddie Murphy's support—even though Arsenio has never given him credit for having lent him a helping hand—was without a doubt one of the reasons behind the Fox decision, albeit too late, to try to hold on to Arsenio.

"Eddie and I talked about this a long time ago," Arsenio once confided, "how this has never happened before, where two black people can be successful, and still be supportive and be cool with each other, like 'Let's fight the power, man.'

"Eddie and I always promised each other that we would never allow women or success to come between us, because that's what happens to blacks," Arsenio continued. "There is a slave mentality in this country that just won't go away. If you can keep black people fighting amongst themselves, you can never have any kind of unity. In unity, there's power and respect in relation to white people.

"I don't think white people will ever respect black people if you don't see them respecting themselves," he continued. "When you see black-on-black crime, you've got to have a low level of respect for those people. That slave mentality is how white people kept the plantations in line. You had black people beat black people. You had Africans sell Africans.

"The sad part is that there are black people who have bought into the game," he continued, "and they get into the mentality of 'I can't be on top of the mountain unless I get rid of Eddie. I can't get into the limelight and get large in television unless I get rid of Arsenio.'

"I've sat around with Stallone many times, and I've never heard him say, 'Unless I get rid of Schwarzenegger, I'll never have a career.' Black people have been taught that there are only a couple of spaces," he concluded, "and you have to kill each other off to have one of those spaces. So we adopt this slave mentality."

Yet despite these words of wisdom and his comments concerning unity the night the Black Pack was born, the truth is that while Arsenio has never torn Eddie Murphy down, he has avoided giving Murphy any credit for having helped launch his career.

In fact, when Arsenio gave his deposition for the Art Buchwald suit against Paramount and was queried about Eddie's reputed gargantuan ego, he confided he had, indeed, been worried about whether or not Eddie was becoming an out-of-touch star during the making of *Coming to America*.

"There came a point in his life," Arsenio stated, "where if Eddie would say, 'I think I'm going to shit on the stage,' people would say, 'Yeah, that's funny, Eddie, do shit on the stage.' And these were people on his payroll. He realized that a lot of them wouldn't be honest with him anymore because he was Eddie Murphy.

"You watch his life change," Arsenio said of Eddie, "and you watch people blast and attack him. People only see the person going back to the curtain and waving good-bye. I saw the other side, the tough side."

If there was a lesson to be learned from watching Eddie Murphy's ego being inflated by his entourage, Arsenio never grasped it. If he had, he would have given credit to Murphy for having opened the Paramount gates for him. But instead Arsenio has been consistently defensive whenever it has been suggested that he was doing well because of the Murphy connection.

"Yes, I'm a friend of Eddie's, but so is Joe Piscopo," he once angrily pointed out. "Being associated with Eddie doesn't mean success. Talent means success, and I have plenty of it."

It is a line to which Arsenio has clung, even though it has been obvious to everyone in La La Land that Murphy was, indeed, instrumental in Arsenio's success. Yet as recently as early 1992, Arsenio was still denying that Murphy had in any way been responsible for his success.

"Eddie's like the brother I never had, but what put me on the map was Joan Rivers losing her job," he was still insisting.

Perhaps, subliminally, Arsenio resents Eddie's movie-star stature, a quality that, despite his TV fame, Arsenio has yet to acquire. Unlike the rarefied strata of movie stardom, TV popularity is borne out of familiarity. And familiarity can breed contempt. With his ego, it is not unlikely that Arsenio would prefer to be above the crowd rather than a part of it. Perhaps that is why a movie career has now become so appealing to him. Whether he admits it to himself or not, Arsenio apparently wants the same deference displayed toward him that fans exhibit toward Eddie.

Take the time Arsenio accompanied Eddie to Hawaii, where he was promoting his concert film *Raw*.

On the plane, fans would tiptoe around Eddie, who was sleeping, to talk to Arsenio, whom they would slap on the back like an old friend and ask for an autograph without reservation. One lady, Arsenio later recalled, asked for his autograph, left, then returned and whispered to him: "I don't want to disturb Mr. Murphy, but tell him I love his work."

"With Eddie, it's like this big movie star," Arsenio said. "They see him once a year, and he's fifty feet tall. With me, they think they know me. The way they come up to me, you'd think that they slept with me every night. Arsenio is always Arsenio and Eddie is always Mr. Murphy."

It was during this stay in Hawaii, Arsenio would later confide, that he first realized he, too, was a celebrity.

"Eddie and I were in Hawaii . . . and I had some time off," he explained. "So we're going to hang out, and we're at a red light and a hooker looks in the window and says, 'Arsenio Hall! I loves you!' She starts crying, 'You have no idea! Not only do I watch you every night, but they show you the next day, and I watch you twice.

"'At night when I watch you, I get my ass beat because my pimp wants me on the streets making money. I get my ass beat for you! That's how much I love you!' I knew then," he laughed, "that I was either a star or I had the potential to become one because I would not take an ass-whipping from a man named Sweet Meat for no talk-show host."

If Arsenio's lack of thanks and recognition of his talents bothered him, Murphy never displayed it. Instead he remained one of Arsenio's staunchest fans. "Arsenio Hall, offstage, is the funniest person I've ever met in my life. He's the only person who can make me laugh until it gets dangerous," Eddie told *Rolling Stone* in February 1989, only a month after "The Arsenio Hall Show" had debuted.

"He has the fastest mind and a knack for recalling obscurities, weird names from the past that make you giggle. I always thought that as soon as Arsenio started being Arsenio, he would take off. And that's what's happened."

For his part, although he has never been quoted regarding Eddie Murphy's talent to amuse, Arsenio has risen to defend Eddie whenever the need presented itself.

"Eddie and I, we fight constantly," Arsenio once explained. "We argue on the way to places and have a ball when we get there. It's one of the reasons we hang out a lot. But you know how brothers are. You can fight, but nobody else better fuck with Eddie. If you come and try to get in the middle of our fight . . . we'll hurt you."

While that may be true of Eddie and Arsenio, it certainly hasn't been true of the other Black Pack members. By 1988, there was already dissension in the ranks. And by 1992, there was no longer any facade of camaraderie between most of the former members.

"The whole Black Pack thing is a weird area," Arsenio conceded. "I like it because it ended a certain kind of jealousy I saw happening. I think it's good these guys work together. But," he added, "a lot of people resent it. And, really, who is the Black Pack? Is it any black guy who's making six figures? Any guy that goes to a disco with us?"

The first member to fall out of favor with Eddie and Arsenio was Robert Townsend, who had been less than flattering in his comments about Eddie while promoting *Raw*, the 1989 concert film he and Eddie had collaborated on.

Ever protective of his best friend, Arsenio was quoted as saying: "One night I turned on the TV and Robert was tearing up a poster of Eddie, saying 'Move over Eddie Murphy.'" Angry at what he perceived to be Townsend's less-than-grateful behavior toward Eddie, Arsenio then accused Townsend of cribbing a skit he and screenwriter Paul Mooney, another Black Packer, had written and putting it in *Hollywood Shuffle* without crediting either of them.

"Robert steals most of the material he uses," Arsenio said adding that, at that point, the Black Pack was nothing more than "a lot of people who won't sue each other."

And, of course, it was Keenen Wayans whom Arsenio had accused of usurping an Eddie Murphy idea and turning it into the movie *I'm Gonna Git You Sucka!* In early 1989, Wayans and Hall were still good friends. "Arsenio is an extremely driven person," Wayans told a reporter, adding, "In some cases that drive tends to make him crazy when he's not where he wants to be. He gets consumed with his idea of success—though I don't really know what his idea of success is."

It may have been Arsenio's less-than-gracious finger pointing at both Townsend and Wayans that ultimately led Wayan's to produce his devastating parodies of Arsenio on "In Living Color" the following year. After all, Wayans and Townsend had been friends since meeting in an audition line at the Improv in New York City, when both were young hopefuls starting out on what they'd expected would be a career as stand-up comics. They were, and continue to be, tight friends, not unlike Arsenio and Eddie.

So Wayans continued his devastating parodies of Arsenio, until the talk-show host finally felt compelled to explain his interviewing techniques to an inquisitive press.

"I try to ask questions that the people who are watching me would," he confided to several newspaper writers. "I'm not Ted Koppel. Every show has a personality and instead of justifying or defending it, this is my show, and it does well. Koppel does what he does. Letterman does what he does and I do what I do. I'm always prepared.

"The reality of show business is that people don't come on the show because they like me," he continued. "They come on because they've got work. What I do is try to find a comfortable balance—try to keep it light and fun. At the same time they know what the deal is. We'd be naive to think that people come on talk shows to talk. They come on to promote a product."

But it was the arguments, some public, some not, within the ranks of the so-called Black Pack, not Wayans's parodies, that ultimately led Arsenio to claim he'd never actually been a member of the pack.

"Eddie used that terminology Black Pack, like I was

supposed to be in this fraternity, and I didn't even know most of those people. I was never a Black Pack member, it was just a lot of publicity," he said in 1990.

Arsenio's comments about the Black Pack were probably true. In attitude Arsenio and Eddie had very little in common with Townsend and Wayans, neither of whom has displayed the same penchant for wine, women, and song. Eddie and Arsenio, however, were self-professed charter members of the DTA (Don't Trust Anybody) group, whose founding father was their mutual idol, Richard Pryor. Women, they believed, only loved you for your money.

"I don't trust people," Arsenio has explained. "That's just the kind of person I am. I'm the guy who's been through the incidents where your best friend who you love like a brother fucks your girl, so I'm kinda bitter. Like, I was going out with a girl once, and her friend came to me and said, 'Be careful. She's trying to get pregnant.' That's scary shit."

On a couple of occasions, there have been allegations of mistreatment of women by Arsenio. The most recent charge against him was hurled by Andrew Dice Clay, who, after a disagreement with Arsenio last year, claimed to have seen the talk-show host physically abusing a blond girlfriend outside the Comedy Store in the early 1980s. The 1992 Andrew Dice Clay charge marked the second time Arsenio had been accused of roughing up a woman.

According to a 1989 *National Enquirer* story, Arsenio and Eddie Murphy were sued by Bridget Porter, a twenty-four-year-old Inglewood, California, woman who claimed she and a girlfriend were lured for sex to Murphy's $6-million Bel-Air mansion on the false promise that they were going to a party.

According to the tabloid, Bridget and her friend

were dining at Nicky Blair's, a popular Sunset Boulvard, restaurant, when they spotted Arsenio and Murphy dining with friends, one of whom was Larry Johnson, Eddie's personal assistant.

According to court records, Johnson approached the women's table and invited them to accompany Hall and Murphy to the Comedy Store, which they did. Then, after Arsenio had done a comedy bit on stage, the two men invited them to go to Eddie's house "for a party."

The women subsequently drove to Murphy's Egyptian-style, walled, and gate-guarded mansion atop Benedict Canyon, arriving there shortly after midnight. After they had been introduced to Murphy, it quickly became apparent that "we had been invited there for the sole purpose of engaging in sexual activity."

After declining the offer, the two women were told to leave, but just outside Murphy's electronic gate, their car got a flat tire. By that time it was 1:00 A.M., so the women buzzed Murphy's security bell for help.

"For the next forty-five minutes," the suit claims, "Eddie and Arsenio spoke to us in gibberish and in a foreign language through the speaker box. They mocked us and told us to put our private parts in front of the security camera."

Finally, after the women pleaded with the two superstars to call them a tow truck, one of Murphy's security guards drove up to the gate and ordered them to move their "goddamn car." The gates then opened and the two women returned to the house, assuming someone would help them change the flat. Instead one of Murphy's bodyguards appeared and began pushing and shoving the women around.

"He threatened me with the dogs and said I'd be beaten up if I didn't get off the property immediately.

Then Eddie and Arsenio came out and watched while two other men came from the side of the house and began pushing and shoving me."

According to Bridget, "Eddie and Arsenio stood by and did nothing" while she was being attacked. "They've got this image of being nice guys," she said, "but they're really jerks who get their kicks degrading women."

Eight months later, on August 23, 1989, claiming she was still having nightmares as a result of the assault, Bridget Porter filed a lawsuit seeking damages for "intentional infliction of severe emotional distress." The outcome of the case is unclear.

Three years later Arsenio would be faced with the threat of a similar suit, this one by a former secretary. But the case would be settled out of court, leaving no ripple on the wave of popularity Arsenio was riding.

CHAPTER

6

Despite having turned down the Fox offer to helm "the Late Show" and his comments to the contrary to his hometown newspaper, Arsenio still coveted a talk show of his own. He was never more sure of it than the night of July 21, 1988, when he made his first—and only—appearance on "the Tonight Show" with his idol Johnny Carson. He had finally made the guest lineup, not as a comic but as an actor, touting *Coming to America*.

"Sitting down with Johnny was an enormous thrill, and to discover that he had seen me perform on television and thought I was good came as a shock. I could have retired happy that night," Arsenio later reminisced.

Instead of retiring, though, Arsenio realized more than ever just how much he really wanted to be the host of his own late-night talk show. "During the commercials, Johnny started talking about being a magician when he was a kid, because he'd heard I was a magician, and that made me think of something else," he explained. "It was like, wait a minute,

Johnny was a drummer, Johnny was a magician. You were a drummer, you were a magician. It looks to me like this is just supposed to be.

"It was the worst interview I've ever done," he continued. "I was terrible that night, because I was elsewhere. I sat there watching Carson do his show and realized how much I missed it, how for the rest of my life I'd dream of being Johnny. Right then I decided I had to do another show. I had to make the dream come true and try and become the Johnny Carson of the nineties."

The following day Arsenio reportedly had his manager, Bob Wachs, telephone Paramount and convince them to underwrite a twenty-six-week commitment for a syndicated talk show. Thus, only two days after Arsenio's "Tonight Show" appearance, Paramount announced it would be producing and distributing a talk show starring Arsenio Hall in 1989.

It's a great story, but alas, like so many of Arsenio's stories, it's simply not true. According to Wachs, he and his partner, Mark Lipsky, had conducted extensive negotiations with Paramount on behalf of Arsenio from February until July 1988, when they finally managed to hammer out a contract with the studio, calling for Arsenio to receive a weekly salary of $50,000 plus a percentage of the syndicated show's profits, which, depending on its ratings, could run between 25 and 45 percent.

It was during this time that Arsenio Hall Communications, Ltd., was born. But only after Arsenio objected to Wachs, Lipsky, and his pal Eddie Murphy formed a company called Eddie Murphy Productions to produce his talk show. With all of the stumbling blocks supposedly removed, the contract with Paramount was signed and Arsenio was on his way to becoming the "Martin Luther King of Comedy," as he once laughingly billed himself.

"I think Dave Letterman is state of the art," Arsenio replied, when asked by the media just where his talk show would fit in. "I've always said that Johnny's the longest, but Dave's the strongest," he laughed, adding, "I'll take anything he'll leave."

Six weeks later Fox Broadcasting filed a lawsuit against him, claiming Arsenio was still under contract to them. "We helped make him a star," grumbled a Fox executive. "He even acknowledged that in interviews. And then he didn't even negotiate with us.

"It's no coincidence Paramount is launching the show in January after our contract with him expires," the exec continued. "But the fact is they negotiated with him before January. We know it's unlikely we'll be able to block production of his show, but it's the principle we're fighting," the exec explained, adding, "Arsenio's angry because he claims we didn't provide him with a wardrobe budget, but we gave him the same as everyone else."

And that was the truth. Arsenio had used his own money, in addition to his $2,000 weekly clothing allowance, for wardrobe expenses during the three months he had hosted "the Late Show" show on Fox. And as he would later explain, "Between buying my clothes and other things that I needed, I just about broke even."

Besides, no amount of complaining by Fox could have dampened Arsenio's spirits. He was too caught up in his vision of the future, of having his very own platform from which to toss his one-liners. "As a comic it can drive you insane when you wake up and you're watching the news and there's Quayle and Gorbachev and Jim and Tammy and you don't have a place to go with all these things going through your mind," he explained. "That's what I've really missed."

As the Fox executive had predicted, the studio was unable to block Arsenio's new show. By the time "The Arsenio Hall Show" made its debut on Tuesday, January 3, 1989, three days after his agreement with Fox had elapsed, the suit had been dropped and Arsenio was happily ensconced in a large office in a second-floor wing of Paramount. He had his long-dreamed-of television talk show and a studio contract for more films.

"I was born to do this," he enthusiastically told interviewers. "When I'm in the spotlight, I'm gone. I love it more than anything in the world. When everyone is barking and screaming, it's the best feeling I've ever felt, like a three-point jumper with one second left in the championship game against Boston. It's better than an orgasm.

"Besides, I have a commitment to correcting the wrongs of TV history," he added, referring to his determination to continue his exposure of black performers on the show.

"To be successful as a black man in this country, you have to be bicultural," he continued. "White people can function in a white world and only concern themselves with white things. But a black man has to know it all. I have to be able to understand the ins and outs of Dan Quayle's political life and also understand why James Brown is in jail. But not Johnny [Carson]. He isn't expected to know who wrote 'My Girl' or even what's going on with Nelson and Winnie Mandela. All he has to do is be funny about John Tower."

By the time Arsenio had landed his lucrative deal with Paramount, he allegedly had received offers from ABC, CBS, and HBO to helm talk shows.

"Yeah, the networks could have had me on, and Fox could have kept me on, too, but they have this philosophy at the networks and the ivory towers where they make the decisions for TV and film: they tell black artists that America will not accept them," Arsenio said. "They'll tell you, 'It didn't play well in America, it didn't test well in America.' But the bottom line is that it's not testing well in their minds and on their desks and in their hearts.

"The network presidents were lying. America is fine," he said. "America is more willing to change than the executives are willing to believe. The executives said Arsenio Hall wouldn't work. But America had not been asked. When they WERE asked, they accepted it.

"I think we're finding out America is not as racist as the people running Hollywood," he conluded. "It's the people making decisions in Hollywood who are racist. I know that's a very tough, mean, harsh statement to make, but that's what I really believe. There's a lot more change going on in the hearts and minds of America than in the racist hearts and minds of the people that run Hollywood."

If that's true, then how does Arsenio explain Paramount Studios complete support of his show? He doesn't. He prefers instead to dwell on how Arsenio Hall, an Afro-American, singlehandedly, fought *the system* and won. Take the time he met with representatives from King World, a major television distributor and the company that syndicates "Oprah," when he was looking for someone to underwrite his own talk show.

"They told me, 'There's one black talk show, that's enough,'" Arsenio likes to recall, adding how later, after his show had become a success, "Michael King came up to me at dinner and asked, 'Can I sit and have a drink with you guys?' And I said, 'No, we're busy. There are enough white people at the table.'"

And yet it was Paramount Studios, essentially a white-owned-and-operated company, and Lucie Salhany, a white woman, who put Arsenio in the catbird seat whence this cockiness emanates. And it was a white man, his manager, Bob Wachs, who negotiated with Paramount on his behalf, ultimately getting the studio to sign Arsenio to a multimillion-dollar film and TV contract. When it comes to making money, capitalistic America can be color-blind.

"I wanted him desperately," Salhany, who was then president of Paramount domestic television, later recalled. "He was a star, and the station owners were convinced of that, too. Any skepticism may have been on the part of the establishment, but I think they may have been a little out of touch. I mean, it certainly was a risk—nobody puts a show on the air knowing it's going to work. But there was no question in the minds of the station owners."

As it turned out, the station owners were right. The year of Arsenio Hall had arrived.

"Everyone has always tried to make something out of me," Arsenio said, prior to the show's debut. "I did a show with Dick Clark and they wanted us to be a salt-and-pepper team. I did 'Solid Gold' and they wanted me to be across between Bryant Gumbel and Andy Gibb. The only time I ever succeeded was when I was doing 'the Late Show' and truly Arsenio. So I'm going to be myself and see how it sells."

The show was a hit with both the public and the TV critics. Arsenio "sold" very well.

"I was infatuated with Muhammad Ali as a kid,"

Arsenio said. "I remember his self-confidence. And even he said, 'I didn't really believe it, but that was my best shot, to try to psych everybody out, and in the meantime maybe convince myself.'

"And that's how I feel now, like I'm the greatest. I've got all the tools. I'm prettier than [Pat] Sajak. I'm quicker than Sajak. Late night has not seen anything like me. I'm going to revolutionize the business. I'm the greatest of all time. You'll never forget me. You'll never forget me.

"That's the way I am, man. I'm going to hit them with that punch he hit Liston with. . . ."

Arsenio was so excited on opening night that before delivering his monologue, which would consist mainly of jokes about NBA superstars, he ran off stage to thank the people lined up outside who had tried to get into the show, but couldn't find seats. Then, returning to center stage, Arsenio gave what would become his trademark salutation: "Let the party begin!"

The opening show's guest lineup was a peculiar and eclectic mix—Nancy Culp, formerly of "The Beverly Hillbillies," who sat in with the band (not playing, just sitting), Brooke Shields, Leslie Nielsen, and Luther Vandross, who ended his stint with Arsenio by turning to the audience and exuberantly asking, "Isn't he fabulous? I'm serious. Fabulous!"

As the debut show wound down Arsenio looked at his guests, his studio audience, and then, turning to the camera, confessed they had just witnessed "the most important night of my life."

By the end of the first week, Arsenio had swapped quips with Quincy Jones, Robert Downey, Jr., Whoopi Goldberg, Ted Danson, Victoria Principal, Louie Anderson, Bobby Brown, Brian Bosworth and then–Laker captain Kareem Abdul-Jabbar (né Lew

Alcindor), whom he had the comedic chutzpah to ask: "Do you ever miss the name Lew?"

Pee-Wee Herman, who was then at his zenith, even dropped by for a visit that week, bringing with him a box of Barbie cereal and a naked-babe transistor radio. In a rare moment of television, the two sat cross-legged on the floor, set their cereal bowls on Arsenio's hassock, and munched and chatted, as Pee-Wee turned the radio's nipple knobs, trying to tune in an appropriately cool station by which to read his Barbie magazine.

In the weeks that followed, Arsenio quickly made a name for himself by delivering a nightly onslaught of naughty sex jokes, toilet humor, and irreverent jabs at everything black—from its culture to its superstars like Michael Jordan and Michael Jackson. He no longer answered to "Little Money," the nickname he was given (to Eddie's "Big Money" moniker) during the filming of *Coming to America*. At that point, Arsenio had become his own man and had given himself his own nickname. In the future, he said, he was to be called the "A-Man."

"I knew I'd hit," Arsenio confided to a reporter not long after his show debuted. "White America only gets uptight when a black guy moves in next door, dates your daughter, or becomes your boss. They've always let us entertain them."

The format of Arsenio's show was invariably the same. Following his monologue, he would segue to the couch for far-ranging, often inane conversations with the likes of Jesse Jackson, who'd munch on chicken wings and talk about third-world debt, or Dr. Ruth Westheimer, whom Hall asked, "Have you ever faked an orgasm?" Unlike many of his guests, who would rise to the occasion, Dr. Ruth did not answer and did not squirm. The guest list was as varied as the topics of discussion.

"We've always partied separately in this country," Hall explained, referring to his audience, which he considered representative of the melting pot of America. ""White kids had 'American Bandstand.' Black kids had 'Soul Train.' The only thing we did together was riot. Now I'm inviting everyone over to my house to jam—and they're coming."

And, indeed, they were. The ratings of "The Arsenio Hall Show" were the highest of any talk show in the history of late night television, other than those of "the Tonight Show."

"My show is a show for everybody," Arsenio repeatedly explained to journalists. "It's what America is really about, because it brings you all of America, as opposed to only a part of it, which is how I grew up watching TV.

"When I was a kid," he continued, "you could watch Johnny Carson for a month and only see one black person. But life is an exchange of cultures, and that's what makes us who we are. The reality of it is that I'm here for young people who are looking for somebody to liberate the bland."

By the end of his first six months on the air, Arsenio had proclaimed himself "Mr. Happy." And why not? "The Arsenio Hall Show" by then had surpassed both Pat Sajak, who was CBS's answer to Johnny Carson for the blink of an eye, and NBC's David Letterman in the ratings. More important, Arsenio's show ranked number one with Madison Avenue's most desired under-thirty-five audience.

"I've worked all my life preparing for this, putting together a platform—my kind of guests, my kind of music, what I think is funny," Arsenio proclaimed. "I've been warming up in the eighties, but I'm really for the nineties. I'm the talk show host for the MTV generation."

Whatever euphoria Arsenio experienced from his newly acquired star status quickly dissipated, however, when he found himself embroiled in a highly publicized controversy with Willis Edwards, who was then president of the Beverly Hills/Hollywood chapter of the NAACP.

The controversy began when Edwards sent Marla Kell Brown a November 8, 1988, letter in which he claimed the NAACP chapter had received "numerous phone calls and complaints" regarding Arsenio's hiring practices. Edwards requested a meeting to discuss this issue. In response to the letter, Arsenio set up a November 30, 1988, meeting, which took place in his office at Paramount and was attended by Edwards; John Forbes, head of the Black Producers Union; Sherry Ford, the executive secretary of the NAACP; Shirley Moore, president of the Association of Black Entertainment Technicians (ABET); and various Paramount executives, as well as Bob Wachs, Mark Lipsky, and Marla Kell Brown.

The discussion, which was heated at times, centered on Arsenio's failure to hire more black technicians on his show. One of the main concerns of Edwards, Ford, and Moore was that Arsenio had six writers on his staff and all of them were white.

Arsenio's contention was that it was his show, he would hire whom he wanted, and he was hiring the best people he could find, regardless of race. "It's unfair for someone to put me in the position where I have to change two hundred years of oppression in my first week of being on the air," he would later say, essentially reiterating what he had told Edwards and the others during the November meeting.

"These are people who have been with me from the beginning," he added, pointing out that while his producer, director, and publicist were white women, his talent coordinator, stage manager, and wardrobe director were black.

The meeting ended on a fairly cordial note. However, according to later depositions by Arsenio and Wachs, Edwards drew Wachs aside shortly before departing, told him that everything would "turn out all right," and then, according to Wachs, explained that the NAACP chapter "needed $40,000" for its twenty-first annual Image Awards ceremony. It was, Wachs would later testify, his "clear impression" that Edwards was suggesting "The Arsenio Hall Show" contribute that amount of money to the NAACP coffers.

When Arsenio heard about the conversation from Wachs, he exploded and refused to attend the Image Awards ceremony, which was scheduled to be held in mid-December. Then, on December 8, 1988, Willis Edwards sent Arsenio a letter on NAACP stationery apologizing "for any misunderstanding" that might have occurred at the meeting. At that point, Arsenio agreed to attend the awards ceremony, where he, Jesse Jackson, Whoopi Goldberg, Michael Jackson, and Eddie Murphy were each given awards for having contributed to the improved image of African Americans.

Despite his letter of apology, however, shortly after the awards ceremony Edwards issued a press release charging Arsenio with discrimination against blacks in his hiring practices and attitudes. The *Los Angeles Sentinel*, a black newspaper, ran the NAACP release on January 5, 1989, with a headline shouting

NAACP BLASTS ARSENIO'S NEW SHOW.

Arsenio was justifiably furious. Not only had he no inkling that Edwards was going to send out such a press release, the *Sentinel* had not even bothered to contact him to get his side of the story.

In an attempt to set the record straight and refute the charges, Arsenio agreed to be interviewed by two of the paper's reporters, Sheena Lester and Gene Johnson, a week later. He met with them in the green room on Paramount's Stage 29 lot on January 12, 1989. The results of his efforts were published in a *Sentinel* story, which carried the headline, HALL: NAACP PRESIDENT "AN EXTORTIONIST."

According to the story, Arsenio had called Edwards a "fuckin' extortionist" who had attempted to wring $40,000 from him for the NAACP and for himself. The *Sentinel* story also quoted Arsenio as saying he had received information that Edwards had sought money in a similar manner from Johnny Carson and/or Carson Productions.

"Find out how much Ed Weinberger has given to Willis Edwards recently," Arsenio had vehemently insisted, "and see if he's been fucked with. See if Johnny Carson's been fucked with. See if Carson Productions gave some money."

Edwards held another press conference and claimed that Arsenio had been "on a campaign to dog my name." Edwards then filed a $10 million libel suit, alleging Hall wrongfully accused him of being an "extortionist."

Later, in their depositions, the two reporters would concede that they had "utilized words of their own choosing" in bringing the story to life. By then, however, the damage had been done.

The fact that he had the Image Award prominently placed in his Paramount office was a constant reminder to Arsenio of just how outraged he was by the implication that he had a bias against African Americans. "It's so depressing," Arsenio confided to friends, "to find that my biggest obstacle didn't turn out to be what people said: 'You're young, you're black, you're going against the legend—Carson.' The biggest stumbling block turned out to be my black organization, the NAACP."

Amazed as well as angry at the lack of support, not to mention the problems, he was enduring at the hands of the local black community, Arsenio sought the advice of Bill Cosby and Jesse Jackson, both veterans of the celebrity game. They each told him the same thing: "Trust your heart. Decide what you're doing is your best effort, and don't let too many people tell you what to do."

Heeding their advice, Arsenio released a statement regarding the charges leveled at him. "I've gone out of my way to make sure I've been fair to everybody," he said. And he denied Edwards's claim that the NAACP had received complaints from all over Los Angeles about his hiring practices.

Arsenio subsequently did an April 1989 *Rolling Stone* interview with Patrick Goldstein in which he reiterated those charges and called Edwards a "phony motherfucking-black-tennis-shoe pimp," and again accused Edwards of demanding a $40,000 donation to the NAACP from him. In return, Arsenio said, Edwards had said he would agree to stop pressuring him about his supposed failure to hire black writers, directors, and producers for his show.

Willis Edwards went ballistic.

"I'm not a pimp," he exploded. "I've never extorted

a penny from anyone. Arsenio's going to have to prove these things in court."

With that, Edwards had filed a second $10 million libel suit, naming Jann S. Wenner, publisher of *Rolling Stone*, writer Goldstein, and Arsenio as defendants.

"My manager told me not to be angry, but I am," Arsenio said about the suit. "I resent the fact that I have to be whiter to be a star. And then there are the jabs from my own people, the implication that I have to be unfair to whites to make blacks happy.

"So, yes, I am angry," he concluded. "I'm on a tightrope and people are punching me from every direction."

Edwards' first libel suit was dismissed in May 1991 by a Superior Court judge on the grounds of "expression of free speech." However, Edwards determinedly appealed, and the California Court of Appeals reinstated the case in September 1991. That decision was upheld by California's highest court in January 1992. And as of November 30, 1992, the second defamation suit was still pending despite Arsenio's bid to have it dismissed.

"What drives me crazy," Arsenio said, "is you look in the mirror and say, 'Your job is making people laugh.' Why the controversy and the pain? I'm just a guy trying to do something good."

The Edwards case was an odd, somewhat bitter experience for Arsenio, whose talk show was then also being criticism by many members of the television press, such as Tom Shales, the Pulitzer Prize–winning TV columnist for *The Washington Post*, for being "too black" for mainstream America.

"Am I being an old fuddy-duddy if I don't get it?" Shales wrote of the Hall show. "If I watch a show like this, one that I feel is for and about black people, then I feel, well, this wasn't meant for me. I've been excluded."

At the same time the middle-aged white Shales was penning his indictment of the show, Hall was under attack by the black press for his TV persona, which they found "embarrassing," especially his "kissing up to second-rate white stars of the Brooke Shields–Eric Roberts ilk," as black journalist Barry Michael Cooper wrote in a lengthy *Village Voice* article.

In September 1989, Dr. Charles King, head of Atlanta's Urban Crisis Center, a think tank dealing with race, was quoted as saying "Hall's eye-rolling and fondness for toilet humor only increase white America's appetite for black buffoonery. As long as we keep them laughing, we're popular," King continued. "Hall's just dancing to white America's tune. If he had some courage, he'd use his show to present black role models who don't earn their living making white people cheer."

Besieged from both sides, Arsenio responded with "They're right when they say my interviews with Muhammad Ali, Joan Collins, or Sammy Davis seem more like tributes than interviews. I'm throwing a party on my show. And when you invite people over for a party, you don't cross-examine them. What do these people want?" he asked. "When I have Stallone on my show, am I supposed to say, 'Yo, Sly, you say you're not a stupid—, yet you marry this crazy bitch who sends you her pictures in the mail, she takes you to the cleaners, she Martinizes you. . . .'

"I could do that, I suppose, but I won't," Arsenio continued. "I'm the 'Candy Man,' doing my best to spread love and laughter. So instead of crackin' on my guests, I'll dance to Motown with Maury Povich. If people want the other shit, let 'em watch 'Crossfire.'"

Looking back at the events surrounding the debut of his show, Arsenio would later concede, "It was a strange time, a very strange time.

"The important thing, though, was to not implement the same racist mentality that I've complained Hollywood has," he concluded. "The bottom line is that we're no better if we say we're a black company and we're just going to do black things, because that's what white companies did."

In planning his show, Arsenio had vividly remembered what he had learned on "Thicke of the Night" and he was determined to have a balanced team, with strong players in all positions. As the show's executive producer, Arsenio hired a staff in his own image—young and unjaded, some black, some not.

One of the first people he hired was Marla Kell Brown, whose previous credits included "A.M. New York" with Regis Philbin. The two had first met in the summer of 1987, when Kell Brown had produced his thirteen-week guest stint on "the Late Show." After having worked with a bewildering succession of guest hosts until Arsenio took over, Kell Brown had become one of Arsenio's most avid supporters, a cheerleading position she continues today as his co-writer and producer.

He also hired director Sandi Fullerton, who had worked with him back in the seventies, when she was directing a segment of Don Kirshner's "Rock Concert" series.

Arsenio even handpicked the band. John B. Williams, bassist, and Michael Wolff, keyboardist and Arsenio's musical director, were old friends from his early days on the concert circuit. In fact, Wolff first met Arsenio in 1979 when both were appearing with Nancy Wilson. Arsenio opened her act and Wolff was her pianist.

"He told me then that he was going to have his own talk show someday and that I would be his musical director," Wolff recalled. "He remembered that because he's very loyal. He's also the hardest-working person I have ever met."

As Arsenio's music director, Wolff not only leads the Posse, as Arsenio has dubbed his studio band, but he frequently gets to play Hall's comedic foil as well. "It's delicate ground I exist on," he laughed.

Another holdover from the old days is Daley Pike, Arsenio's warm-up man, whom he first met at the Comedy Cottage in the late 1970s, when he was emceeing the shows. According to Arsenio, he had been so stricken with stage fright during his first appearance at the Cottage that Pike had to introduce him to the audience eight times before he finally coaxed him on to the stage.

"Every night he would start to introduce me, look back, and I'd have disappeared. I would've jumped in my car and driven away," Arsenio now laughs. Of course, Arsenio's recollection differs from that of Ed Hellenbrand, the owner of the Comedy Cottage, who recalls that it was difficult to get Arsenio *off* the stage rather than on.

But then, Arsenio has never been one to spoil a good story. He is, after all, a comedian whose penchant for twisting facts into amusing anecdotes has earned him a magnificent livelihood.

"People didn't get jobs here because they used to work on 'The Mike Douglas Show,'" Kell Brown is fond of saying. "Our attitude was 'If you want a different product, you need different people.'" Still, Arsenio's imprint can be found all over the show, including its theme song, which he supposedly wrote on one of those rare days when he was feeling down. Titled "Hall or Nothing," the lyrics of the song—"It's Hall or nothing, no one else will do. It's Hall or nothing, you'll be mine before I'm through"—are an interesting reflection of Arsenio's belief in . . . himself.

Music has always been a large part of Arsenio's life, which is probably one of the reasons why he spent most of his hiatus from the show that year creating "Chunky A," a three-hundred-pound rapper swathed in a black spandex jumpsuit, with gold chains and a big "A" slung around his neck, who bore a marked resemblance to Arsenio in a full-body padded suit, complete with overly padded rear end.

Billed as Arsenio's older brother, Chunkton Arthur Hall, according to his "official biography," had two passions: women and food. "Arsenio was driven by the need to succeed," claimed the obese rap singer's bio. "Chunky was driven by the need to feed." A large figment of Arsenio's imagination, Chunky was Arsenio's alter ego. He was created after Arsenio watched women in the audience swoon as Heavy D, a real rap performer, rapped his way into their hearts during a concert one night.

Titled *Large and in Charge*, the MCA album featured cameo performances by Paula Abdul and Wil Wheaton. It hit the music stores on November 21, 1989, preceded a week earlier by a music video directed by Larry Blackmon, lead singer of Cameo. Despite Arsenio's high hopes for Chunky, and his announced plans for a second album, however, it never happened. "Chunky was a fun thing simply because music is like crocheting to me. It's a hobby, as long as you keep your ego intact and realize you are a comedian first and musician second. Besides, my life is much crazier now than it was then and . . . the costume was too hot."

Thus Arsenio turned his attention from rap music to movies. He appeared in a cameo role in *Harlem Nights*, another Eddie Murphy comedy, playing a gangster who "hates Eddie's guts." The movie did poorly at the box office, but Arsenio could have cared less. He refused to do any advance publicity for the film and later confided he had only appeared in the movie because Paramount had counted it as one film in his four-picture deal.

On the TV talk-show front, everything was going better than fine. The ratings were up, the criticisms were down.

"I think I get afraid that maybe some kind of Caucasian talk-show Mafia is going to put out a hit man on me," Arsenio quipped, "and I'll find Ed McMahon's head in my bed or something."

By the end of 1989, Arsenio could well afford to joke about his success. He was holding court in Lakers owner Jerry Buss's private box at the Los Angeles Forum, and hobnobbing with the great and would-be great. More important, his number of television outlets had climbed from an initial 160 to 205 and the show ranked number one among the under-thirty-five audience so coveted by advertisers. "It's a phenomenon," heralded Lucie Salhany, president of Paramount Domestic Television.

There could be no doubt in anyone's mind that Arsenio had traveled a far distance from 1988, when the biggest publicity piece on him had been a *USA Today* weekend magazine color layout of his stuffed animal collection, which then included 250 teddy bears of all sizes and descriptions. By the beginning of 1990, there was hardly a newspaper who hadn't written something about America's first black late-night talk-show host. Arsenio's face graced the covers of numerous major magazines, and he was the focus hundreds of interviews. Everyone, it seemed, was interested in Arsenio Hall.

"My success isn't a race thing," he told reporters. "It's an age thing. This is something the white press has never understood. They bet big money I wouldn't make it. They said a black show just wouldn't play in white-bread America. They said it so often I started to worry maybe they were right."

But they weren't right. Arsenio Hall was a phenomenon whose time had arrived. He had fulfilled his childhood fantasy beyond his wildest dreams. He had his own talk show and he had become a household name—a celebrity among celebrities.

"I'm going to keep on doing this show," he crowed to the press, "until everyone cries uncle and I'm the undisputed king of late night."

Yet to another writer he admitted, "I have this strange paranoia. I guess I don't want people to get mad at me. I feel very black and very alone, and I don't want to ruffle the feathers of the white establishment with my success. I just like to present some entertainment and stay low-key. I don't want my success to irritate anyone. When you start winning, they don't like you as much."

In a relatively short time Arsenio Hall had become a winner. And he was right. There were those who didn't like him and a lot of what they didn't like was Arsenio's own fault. It had nothing to do with the color of his skin. It had to do with the tone of his humor, and his impulsive, often off-color remarks, such as when, in a guest appearance on the show, actress Sally Kirkland gushed that she thought he was wonderful. "I can tell," Arsenio replied. "Your nipples are hard."

It had to do with his overplayed humility and his frequent bouts of jaw-dropping arrogance, two traits copied from his childhood hero, Muhammad Ali, just as surely as he copied the art of being a talk show host from Johnny Carson, and the oft-practiced flourish signature which, based on that of Dinah Shore, has become one of his several trademarks.

Having become a walking, talking amalgamation of the best he had surveyed via television as a child, is it any wonder that Arsenio is filled with insecurities and fearful that someday, somehow, he will be unmasked and it will all end? Is it surprising that despite his fame and fortune, there's always a little, nagging voice somewhere in the back of his head, constantly reminding him of just how fleeting fame can be?

"One bad show, and I'm mentally packing a U-Haul," he has often admitted. "But I don't want to start playing it safe. I accept the fact that I can't have it forever. Ali was the greatest, but someday someone beat him, and someone beat the guy who beat him.

"When I was in high school, Jimmy Walker was the hottest. Then I saw a cable television special a while back in which people walked by him and joked, 'That's Arsenio Hall,' because I'm hot, and he's not. It's scary. Someday I'll be the punch line."

CHAPTER

7

Only six months after "The Arsenio Hall Show" hit the air, Arsenio found himself embroiled in the first of what would turn out to be several highly publicized feuds between himself and other celebrities. This first one, however, was surprising because it involved filmmaker Spike Lee and, when it first began, had nothing to do with Arsenio.

In an April 1989 edition of the *Los Angeles Times* Calendar section, Lee took Arsenio's pal Eddie Murphy to task for having failed to do his share to help other blacks in the film industry. "I love Eddie Murphy and I'm 100 percent behind him, but if I ever get one iota of the power he has, I'm gonna raise holy f— hell," Lee said in the article. "Eddie has made a billion dollars for Paramount. Yet I don't see any black executives with any real power at that place."

"Eddie," Spike concluded, "needs to flex his muscles in ways that can help black people get into this industry. Clout isn't just getting the best table at Spago. How's that helping your people?"

Upset by Lee's harsh criticism of him, Eddie

responded with "It's real easy to be on the outside looking in, telling people what you should be doing, but I don't need anyone telling me how much social consciousness I should have.

"Progress is a gradual thing in this town," he explained. "We've made light-years of progress in the past five years. And Spike, Keenen, and Robert Townsend are great examples. Ten years ago those guys couldn't have gotten pictures made in this town. But since I've had success at the box office, every studio has been looking around for a black guy of their own who could make hit movies.

"I don't think the answer is me rushing into Paramount and raising hell," he continued. "You can't go into someone's house and start yelling just because you're Eddie Murphy. It's their house. Clout comes and goes around here. I'm just the brother of the moment.

"I've made lots of contributions to help my people prosper. But I'm not a politician. I'm a businessman and a filmmaker. I've opened the door for Spike and now he's throwing rocks at me," Murphy had laughingly concluded.

Arsenio was stunned by Lee's criticism of Murphy because, as he said, "No one is closer to me than Eddie and he's never said a negative thing about the man. When we talk about young filmmakers, it's Spike's work we respect because he's got courage."

Arsenio remained above the fray until Lee appeared as a guest on the June 30, 1989, edition of his show to promote his new film *Do the Right Thing*, and not only blasted Murphy again for not hiring more blacks on his films but even went so far as to mock Whoopi Goldberg's blue-tinted contact lenses.

At that point, Arsenio got involved in what was

turning out to be a fascinating meeting of black cultural opposites. Born into an intellectual, middle-class family, Lee had already become famous for outspoken films; Arsenio was, the product of poor parent's and a broken home, and had gained his fame by learning to swim in the mainstream. There was no way the two were going to see eye-to-eye.

As Arsenio would so aptly put it months later, "I'm the son of a Baptist preacher. I know what I know. I was brought up in a house where they said, 'Try to kill them with love.' My computer has been programmed more like Martin Luther King's program: if it ends in a fight, you blew it."

And therein lies a major difference between Arsenio Hall and Spike Lee. There appear to be only two major routes for American black artists to follow. They can either hurl nasty epithets at the Establishment with righteous indignation, or they can go with the flow of mainstream America.

It is not by happenstance that Spike chose to bring the life of Malcolm X to the big screen last year, or that Arsenio, who grew up believing the doctrines of Martin Luther King, chose to jump into mainstream American television. It is a battle of philosophies dating back to the sixties, a battle no one can win because there is no right, no wrong. Lee will be criticized as being too militant, too black. And Arsenio has already found himself in the middle of controversy, with white America claiming his show is too black and black America claiming his show is too white, that he has sold out and is the nineties' answer to Uncle Tom.

While it's a difficult balancing act, Arsenio seems to be able to successfully walk the wire. Like Bill Cosby, Whoopi Goldberg, Eddie Murphy, and other

African-American celebrities, Arsenio has managed to attain success by playing mostly on Establishment terms while still retaining his blackness.

He is walking a tight rope. He belongs everywhere and yet, at the same time, belongs nowhere. It is a dilemma facing most successful blacks, unless they happen to be a Spike Lee, bursting with hostility and black pride. For Lee there is no middle road. For Arsenio there is nothing but a middle road. And never the twain shall philosophically meet.

At the conclusion of Lee's appearance on his show, Arsenio invited him back to assess the impact of *Do the Right Thing* on the American moviegoing public. Lee agreed to reappear and returned to New York, where only days later he told an audience attending a new music seminar titled "Afrocentricity: The Revolution Must Be Marketed" that Arsenio was an Uncle Tom, who is "hugging white women every minute," that Eddie Murphy had "no black consciousness," and that Whoopi Goldberg "wants to be white."

Lee also accused Arsenio of having him on his talk show only so that he could "assassinate me."

When Spike called Arsenio a few weeks later to confirm his upcoming appearance on the show, Arsenio asked him about the comments. According to Arsenio, Spike said, "I never said anything negative about you guys there." Attributing the stories to "some wonderful Caucasian journalist creating lies to make black people fight," Arsenio hung up the phone.

Two days later, however, Arsenio was watching MTV and saw "a film clip in which he [Spike] was saying everything he said he didn't say." Infuriated, Arsenio attacked Lee a week later during an interview on the syndicated radio show *Radioscope*. "Sometimes Spike has a blacker-than-thou attitude," Arsenio told listeners, "but Spike is no blacker than any of the people he criticizes—Bill Cosby, Oprah Winfrey, Eddie Murphy. I know what Spike's game is. He's the new Malcolm and everyone else is a money-grubbing hustler," Arsenio said. "It's BS, that's what it is. Spike would love to have my audience. He'd love to have Eddie's audience. Me and Eddie have become targets for people like Spike.

"To talk behind my back and constantly criticize me instead of going about his business is not the way to go," he concluded. "Maybe we'll see how much ghetto Spike has in him 'cause next time I'm going to whip his ass. I ain't going to ask him no more."

Four days later Spike did his own *Radioscope* interview. "I've never gone behind Arsenio's back, dogging him out," he responded. "If anything, he tried to dog me out when I was a guest on his show. I think it's unfortunate for him to get out in the media and say he's going to 'whip my ass.' I thought more of the brother than to say something like that.

"Arsenio has my number," Lee concluded, "and I know he has a telephone. So if he heard I was saying stuff behind his back, he should've called me up. But he didn't. He's fallen prey to the same stuff he's chastising me for."

By the end of the summer all was cool between the two brothers once again. Arsenio, as has become his pattern, not only backed off the issue but switched directions.

"I defended Whoopi and Eddie on the air because I have a habit of defending people I respect if I think someone is wrong in attacking them," Arsenio admitted, adding, "and I got myself into a public battle. It was probably a big mistake because a lot of people think I hate Spike. But there was never an issue of controversy between Arsenio Hall and Spike Lee. He never said anything about me. If anything, I was nosy and wasn't minding my own business and got into a public debate," Arsenio would later explain, once again rewriting history in the process.

Several months after their very public disagreement, Spike and Arsenio found themselves coaching rival teams (Arsenio the away players, Lee the home team) at Magic Johnson's Midsummer Night's Magic, an annual charity all-star basketball game in Los Angeles. Although they remained distant from each other, the two shook hands before and after the game. "We're not going to be best friends," Lee said later, adding "but we never were best friends."

For his part Arsenio regretted his actions, which he attributed to "immaturity." "I responded like a kid from the ghetto in Cleveland instead of like the executive producer of "The Arsenio Hall Show," he said. "It was very important for me to shake Spike's hand at the game and let him know it wasn't like that."

Not long after that, Eddie Murphy was quoted in a *Rolling Stone* interview. "Spike," Murphy said, "gets overanxious playing that militant brother role and occasionally says some stupid stuff."

When Spike's blockbuster film *Malcolm X,* had its premiere in mid-November 1992, all apparently was forgiven, at least publicly. Spike appeared on Arsenio's show and a night or two later, when Elton John and Bernie Taupin were guests, Arsenio wore one of Lee's Malcolm X baseball hats, a subtle way of once again making peace with the outspoken director.

Not every feud involving Arsenio's show has made it into the headlines, of course. There was the time, for instance, not long after the show had debuted, when Little Richard so infuriated a member

Alan Thicke, with Arsenio at a 1988 Kings hockey game, claims to admire his former second banana's "killer instinct." *Photo credit: © Celebrity Photo Agency*

Arsenio realized a childhood dream on November 7, 1990, when he received his star on the famous Hollywood Walk of Fame as his mother, Annie, proudly watched. *Photo credit: © Celebrity Photo Agency*

Arsenio and "Dynasty" actress Emma Samms were a romantic twosome but, Arsenio admitted, "Dating white women is not smart, career-wise." *Photo credit: © Celebrity Photo Agency*

Arsenio and his close friend, Earvin "Magic" Johnson share a love of wine, women, and basketball. Here they are seen at the press conference to announce the production of Magic's safe sex Paramount video. *Photo credit: © Celebrity Photo Agency*

Arsenio's large Paramount office reflects his love of television, basketball, and his own celebrity status.
Photo credit: Eddie Sanderson—Shooting Star.

Arsenio and Eddie Murphy have been like brothers since they first met in 1983. Yet they reportedly had a falling out in the summer of 1992. *Photo credit: Erik Heinila—Shooting Star*

Roseanne Arnold and Arsenio spent almost a year warring with each other after the talk show host joked about her weight once too often. *Photo credit: Globe Photos*

Paula Abdul and Arsenio were a brief Hollywood "item," but the twosome claimed they were nothing more than friends in 1989. *Photo credit: Lester Cohen— Shooting Star*

Arsenio was a struggling comic in Chicago when this 1979 publicity photo was taken. A short while later Nancy Wilson helped him move to the West Coast. The rest is history. *Photo credit: Courtesy of Melba Caldwell*

Arsenio and Jay Leno were friends when this photo was snapped in 1990. The following year, after Leno was tapped to replace Johnny Carson, Arsenio denied the two were friends and a bitter feud ensued. *Photo credit: Globe Photos*

of Arsenio's audience by his preening and prancing around the stage, crying "Ain't I pretty?," that absolute mayhem ensued.

"You soft, man," yelled a man in the audience. "You ain't no real man. You soft."

"Shuddup!!" Little Richard screamed back. "I've got a girlfriend. I've got lots of girlfriends. I'm more of a man than you'll ever be!"

Stunned, Arsenio sat there, next to actress Markie Post, watching his show gallop away from him. After the show he admitted he had sat there, watching the argument, "feeling more Caucasian than she did." Although the cameras had been running throughout the melee, the segment was later edited down, and the public was none the wiser.

Despite his armistice with Spike, life for Arsenio in 1989 was not about to return to normal. Instead, he had two frightening experiences that dramatically changed his life.

The first incident occurred not long after the murder of 21-year old actress Rebecca Schaeffer by John Bardo, an obsessed fan, in late July, 1989. Schaeffer's murder caused a major panic within the Hollywood community because Bardo had managed to track her down at her home, shooting her to death when she simply answered the ringing doorbell. The Schaeffer case created a wave of business from celebrities for L.A.'s private security companies, most of whom charge an average of $225,000 for full-time protection.

But in mid-1989 Arsenio did not employ private security. It was, at least at that point, the farthest thing from his mind. By the end of 1989, however, he'd changed his mind and now employs round-the-clock bodyguards. What changed his mind about security that year was a possible kidnapping plot gone awry.

As Arsenio would later recall, he had arrived at Los Angeles International airport one evening and had been met at the arrival gate by a man in a trench coat who looked like he would have been a limo driver. The man approached him. "He called me by name and announced he was my driver," Arsenio recalled.

Quickly taking Arsenio's carry-on suitcase, the two started down the airport corridor together. Then another man, this one in a black suit and carrying a sign that read "Hall" on it, approached Arsenio and introduced himself as his driver. Arsenio turned to the first man just in time to see the fellow drop the suitcase and fled into the crowd.

"I've always wondered if the guy was a fan, or someone who wanted to kidnap me," Arsenio later explained. Whatever the answer, since that experience, he insists on one driver, someone he knows by sight. "I won't use anybody else. I've become paranoid."

Adding to his paranoia only a short while later was the first of what turn out to be many death threats against him, all of which would be telephoned in to Paramount Studios. Such was the case on a night in September, 1989, when the switchboard operator at Paramount received a call from a man, who said he was calling to warn Arsenio.

Two of his friends were on their way from San Francisco to Los Angeles to kill Arsenio because they were jealous of his friendship with Paula Abdul, whom Hall had been dating and had dubbed "the last good girl in Hollywood." Adding to the ominous tone was the caller's statement that the men were on crack.

Studio security was immediately increased, with armed security guards and the police patrolling the Paramount lot in twenty-four-hour shifts. But the two would-be assassins never appeared.

Arsenio subsequently turned the story into an amusing anecdote for the press, saying: "I wasn't worried about dying. What worried me most was my demographics. I thought, 'Wait a minute. Is my show appealing to baseheads?' I wanted some Boston college professor, or an aggressive pre-law student from Detroit, watching. Instead there's a party of rockheads in the Bay Area who watch me every night and have decided to kill me!"

But beneath the humor there was fear. It was the beginning of Arsenio's paranoia, which was heightened not long after that call by yet another telephone warning having again to do with his relationship with Paula Abdul. This time the call was from a member of the Crips, one of L.A.'s most notorious street gangs, who was calling to warn Arsenio that two gang members were seriously considering "blowing" him "away."

The following evening, Arsenio found he was being trailed by a mysterious BMW only seconds after he pulled out of the Paramount lot and began heading west on Melrose Avenue. The car followed him through West Hollywood and Santa Monica, up the Pacific Coast Highway, past Malibu to Zuma Beach.

Convinced the Crips were coming to get him, Arsenio later confided he was "scared shitless" as he raced along at eighty mph in his white Jaguar, with the BMW in close pursuit.

Forced finally to stop at a red light, Arsenio watched in terror through his rearview mirror as the BMW pulled up behind the him and a head popped up through the sunroof. Much to his relief, however, it wasn't an Uzi-bearing Crip. It was a car full of girls, giggling and yelling their undying love and admiration for him. Relieved that his life was to be spared, but disgusted by the situation, Arsenio floored the Jag and managed to leave his surprised pursuers in a swirl of Malibu sand.

Since then, he has received death threats from a variety of sources—from disgruntled L.A. gang members to members of the Klu Klux Klan—but Arsenio is prepared for the worst . . . now. He no longer goes out in public without at least one body-guard at his side. He has also been known to carry a gun, usually tucked in the back waistband of his pants, be they jeans, sweats, or expensive tailored slacks, and his hillside home is an armed fortress with the latest state-of-the-art security system.

"I've gotten Klu Klux Klan letters saying I'm a nigger bastard and puppet to the Hollywood Jews," he confided not long ago. "But I don't read a lot of that stuff because it depresses me. Some of it goes to the police, or we alert the pages or Paramount. But for the most part I just ask my assistant to keep all the negative mail away from me."

Not all of Arsenio's mail, of course, has been "negative." Some of it has been positively hilarious, especially the abundant requests from women seeking to meet him.

"I'm surprised by who women see as sex symbols," Arsenio laughingly admitted. "But the letters and Polaroid photos I get of nude women are really strange. I got a gift the other day of a pair of panties and a condom. The note said, 'I'm in the third row. If you want to investigate this gift, let me know.'"

One of the more offbeat proposals, however,

came from a woman who enclosed a snapshot of herself sitting totally nude in the backseat of a car.

Arsenio's response, he later confided, was amazement and then laughter. "I'm looking at this photo, thinking 'Hey, if you want to meet me, don't get in the back of a '74 Buick Electra and take a naked picture.' That's not the girl I'm looking for!"

But the most unusual invitation Arsenio has received to date came from a Laurel Springs, New Jersey, woman who paid more than $4,000 to have an enormous billboard on Sunset Boulevard carry the message: ARSENIO! CARLINE WANTS YOU, followed by her telephone number.

"I was determined to do something original," she explained. "I mean, how does one go about meeting a man like Arsenio Hall?"

Arsenio was so impressed by the billboard that on his August 11, 1992, show he had a shot of it flashed across the screen. But he never called Carline. Or maybe he did and couldn't get through because, according to Carline, in the days following the August 11 telecast of her telephone number, she received dozens of calls, including some from prison inmates who had the audacity to call collect!

Not all of the "negativity" Arsenio tries to elude arrives in the mail, either. A lot of it has, literally, walked through the door, such as when Arsenio found himself in a shouting match with several members of Queer Nation, the gay activist group, during the taping of a December 1991 show.

Angry about a joke Arsenio had made, referring to a Gay Pride parade as a "Gay Country Safari" and suggesting heterosexuals would roll up their windows and lock their car doors as it passed by, several members of the group stood up, just after a commercial break, and accused Arsenio of being homophobic and not booking enough openly gay guests.

"We have a lotta gay guests," Arsenio retorted, "but it's none of your damn business if they're gay."

When the activists continued questioning Arsenio's choice of guests, he exploded. "What's wrong with you, man? I'm black! I'm the biggest minority you know about!

"I don't want to hear any of that trash!," he added. "This ain't 'The Morton Downey Show.'"

Although he managed to keep his rage in check during the taping, Arsenio went fulltilt backstage, screaming, "I'll never be embarrassed like that again. I wanted to punch that guy out."

The confrontation, which lasted about ten minutes, was aired in its entirety after Arsenio, who at first was going to edit it out, decided, "If I dump it, they'll just go to the press and then the whole thing will be blown out of proportion."

"Their accusations were twisted, absurd lies that really bothered me," Arsenio later said. "If I treated them the way they treated me, I'd be a gay basher. I'm a comedian, and I'd be the first not to do a joke if I felt it created some kind of pain for someone. I am not a callous, heartless comic. I've apologized for many things. But I will not apologize to Queer Nation.

"They were complaining about no openly gay celebrity guests," he continued, "and I was saying that if they're not open, that's not my problem. I'm not interested in putting people on because of their sexual preference. It's not my responsibility to introduce certain comedians and singers as 'Ladies and gentlemen, a very funny man, and a homosexual, put your hands together for . . .' That's bullshit, and they can kiss my black ass on that.

"Maybe people within the gay community want to live their lives privately," he added. "I have friends who feel it would be a terrible assault on their career if people knew they were gay. I can name you five singers who are gay and have women crazy about them, and they feel they would be discriminated against. At the same time I have hardworking friends who are activists for gay rights who believe that the Queer Nation approach is detrimental.

"As far as my being homophobic is concerned, that's ridiculous. If I were homophobic, I'd lose half of my staff and a lot of my guests. It's as simple as that."

Nevertheless, not long after his yelling match with the activists, in what was clearly an effort to defuse his gay critics, Arsenio did invite Harvey Fierstein, the openly gay actor and playwright, to be on the show. Wearing a colorful, flowing caftan, Fierstein observed that "Gay people should be allowed to be as dumb and boring as you heterosexuals." It was a sentiment to which Arsenio nodded in agreement.

As it turned out, however, Arsenio's encounter with the gay activists was not over, despite the appearance by Fierstein.

In May 1992, Queer Nation returned a second time to disrupt a taping of Arsenio's show. The group was objecting to Andrew Dice Clay's presence as a guest that night because Clay's comedy consists of material considered by many people to be homophobic, sexist, and racist.

This time, to thwart the disruption, Arsenio met with the activist leaders in his dressing room for a forty-five-minute discussion prior to the show. He then tossed out his opening monologue and, acknowledging the group's presence in the audience, opened a discussion about homophobia, telling the audience that the real problem in Hollywood wasn't people like himself, it was "closeted entertainers and studio executives."

Arsenio followed this with an attempt at a serious discussion with Andrew Dice Clay about whether or not his brand of humor encouraged violence against women and gays. Under fire from Hall, Clay at one point appeared to be on the verge of tears. But his upset quickly turned to anger when, only days later, Clay learned that he would not be welcomed back on Arsenio's show.

"It's been a mistake to have him on the show," Arsenio conceded when asked about Clay's previous appearance. Comparing his humor with Clay's, Arsenio said he believed "you can't go wrong doing jokes about people who support apartheid, or racists, or anti-Semitic politicos like Pat Buchanan. Those are the people I go after, people like F. W. de Klerk, David Duke, George Bush, Don King, and Donald Trump."

As for Andrew Dice Clay, Arsenio decided after the fact that he was adamantly opposed to his brand of humor. "Racism by any name is still racism. I've watched Dice do handicapped jokes that I wouldn't do, and at one time I was like, 'Well, he ain't messing with black people. I'm fine. He's messing with handicapped people and Asian people and gay people and people with AIDS.'

"Sometimes it's hard to see someone else's pain," Arsenio continued. "One day I listened to a tape of Andrew's concert. And some things he said about people with AIDS made me say, 'I've been wrong and irresponsible.' That has nothing to do with Queer Nation and what happened on the show—but I'm responsible for anything I present to America."

Of course, by the time Arsenio came to this decision, Dice Clay had already been a guest on his show six times, which, as the foulmouthed comic later pointed out, was "a lot of times for a guy to make a mistake."

"If Arsenio would have done this two years ago, I would have left it alone," Clay said, adding, "So now you wanna come after me? You who have a hit show? If you come after me, I'm gonna destroy you, Arsenio."

"Yeah, I got letters that said I was too hard on Andrew Dice Clay," Arsenio responded. "And I got other letters that said, 'Thank goodness somebody finally told him off.' It's this simple. For every guy who doesn't like me, there are a lot of people, who do. That's why I'm on the air."

A month after the public brouhaha, Dice Clay put his plan of destruction into operation. While appearing on the Howard Stern radio show on April 20, 1992, he lashed out at Arsenio's hypocrisy, calling him everything from Uncle Tom to a Black Mr. Ed. "I got a lotta black fans, and I'll tell you something about your people Arsenio. The black people, they are completely embarrassed by you. You're an alien to them. They just hate you."

Clay then recalled Arsenio, whom he referred to as Ass-senio, as having a reputation for being mean and short-tempered in his early days as a stand-up comedian.

"You who has the nerve to call me a racist, when on my last HBO special, I talked about how racism is bad and how instead of building barriers, we should break 'em down," Clay began. "You, Arsenio, who doesn't like material on women, after I saw you personally drag a girlfriend of yours out of the Comedy

Store by her hair and slap her around in front of other comics. You said it was a mistake to have me on your show?"

Under prodding from Stern, Clay said, "I saw a few things with him. One night he was dating this girl, who, by the way, was one of these white bleached-blond chicks. And he got mad at her. He was having some kind of argument, and all of a sudden he grabbed her by her bleached-blond hair, and yanked her out of the Comedy Store, and started slapping her around, 'till some comics got in between.

"This is a guy who tries to come on television and say, 'Hey, I'm Mr. America. I'm Mr. Nice Guy. Who I once saw jump into an audience just 'cause a guy heckled him. And beat the crap out of the guy.

"He criticizes me for my act, and then he tries to come on to every broad who goes on his show who has a great body. I have an act, a character, but I've never slapped around a woman," Clay said. "I've had the same girlfriend for six years, and a girl doesn't stay with a guy six years if she's getting punched around."

Having learned his lesson in the past with Willis Edwards and then Spike Lee, Arsenio wasn't about to become embroiled in another public battle. "Arsenio said he wishes Andrew the best of luck with his career. That's all he has to say," was all Dana Freedman, Hall's publicist, would say.

What else could she say? Perhaps his delivery and his platform could have been classier, but Andrew Dice Clay told a chilling tale. He was neither the first nor the last person to witness Arsenio's bad temper.

CHAPTER

8

I f 1989 had been an interesting year for Arsenio, 1990 proved to be even more intriguing, thanks to everything from bomb threats to a major lawsuit to a bitter feud with Roseanne Arnold as well as on-air jousting matches with Madonna and LaToya Jackson. It was also the year that Willis Edwards filed his lawsuit and Bob Wachs and Arsenio had a bitter parting of the ways.

The first hint that 1990 might be an explosive year for Arsenio came not on January 9 when Edwards initially filed his $10-million lawsuit, but when, shortly after the beginning of the New Year, a young man in the audience tried to throw a smoke bomb onto the stage and it broke in his hand, splattering members of the audience. The would-be terrorist wound up with burn holes in his clothes and a year in prison.

Then in late January, Arsenio received a rash of telephone bomb threats, leading plainclothes police and security guards to scour the studio for suspicious packages while an unsuspecting audience howled with laughter during their host's opening monologue.

It had been the ninth time in six months that a mystery man had called to inform the studio receptionist that the show would be blown to smithereens. What was nerve-racking was not that it was always the same caller, but that he knew the exact layout of Stage 29.

"It's frightening," a crew member conceded, "because you can't discount a threat like that. The day you say, 'Oh, it's just him again,' could be the day the whole stage blows up."

The second explosion of the year, however, occurred in February, when Arsenio offended the National Academy of Recording Arts and Sciences by suggesting the Grammy Awards should be renamed the "apartheid awards" because too few black performers were honored in the nationally televised prime-time ceremony. Arsenio was upset because his friend, vocalist Bobby Brown, had been handed his Rhythm-and-Blues Male Vocalist of the Year award during the nontelevised daytime ceremony.

"I think it's safe to say we are outraged," conceded Michael Green, president of NARAS. "Anytime a person in a communications position makes an offhand remark which has racially bigoted overtones to it, it obviously has the potential to be divisive.

"I am appalled that he would make such a comment," Greene added, "because Brown was out of the country on Grammy night."

Nothing more was heard on that subject from Arsenio. Once again he had shot from the hip, and missed.

At that point, however, Arsenio could have cared less. His mind was concentrated on the problems he was having with Bob Wachs and Mark Lipsky, his managers, whom he had just discovered were being paid $5,000 a week as "production executives" on his show.

Arsenio was upset because, as he would later state, the money they were earning was coming out of the show's production budget and, therefore, his pocket, and neither man, in Arsenio's eyes, was providing any services to the show. Confronted by Arsenio, the two men had agreed to no longer draw a salary from the show. However, their names were to remain in the program credits.

By this time Wachs had been in contact with Disney, Warner, and Columbia studios in search of a more lucrative contract than the one X-Management had originally negotiated with Paramount and which was coming up for renewal. Wachs was, of course, also renegotiating with Paramount.

When Disney Studios proposed a $10-million contract, all of it payable upon Arsenio's signature on the dotted line, Wachs immediately went to Paramount, which had been offering a $7-million deal, and used the Disney deal to prod Paramount into offering Arsenio a sixth year on his TV contract (at a healthy $125,000 per week) plus an increase in his net-profit participation in the show.

Although Wachs apparently had wanted to sign with Disney, Lipsky had wanted Arsenio to remain with Paramount. Arsenio had decided to listen to Lipsky. For their efforts, Lipsky and Wachs received a commission of $1,050,000.

Despite the big bucks Wachs had brought into his life, however, Arsenio no longer trusted him. The relationship had been strained since October 1989, when Wachs had unsuccessfully tried to convince Arsenio that they had an oral agreement that X-

Management would receive 50 percent of his earnings. The ensuing revelation of a $5,000 weekly salary had just been one more cinder in Arsenio's eye.

Finally, on August 2, 1990, Arsenio's attorneys sent a letter to X-Management breaking Hall's contract with the company. A week later Arsenio's attorneys filed a suit against Wachs, and his company, X-Management, to retrieve several million dollars in commissions they claimed Wachs had obtained wrongfully from him because, under California state law, neither Wachs nor X-Management was allowed to negotiate employment on behalf of their clients, which Wachs, of course, had been doing since wooing Arsenio away from Roy Gerber with a supposed promise of $1 million.

It is unclear whether or not Arsenio had known Wachs could not legally negotiate on his behalf during the three years the two had worked together. But what is clear is that Wachs and Lipsky had played a major role in making Arsenio a multimillionaire.

In the three years since Arsenio had bid Gerber and Gilbert adieu, X-Management had negotiated not only Arsenio's four-picture deal with Paramount, but also the production of "The Arsenio Hall Show" as well as the Fox "Late Show" contract.

As it turned out, court documents would reveal Wachs had known that Eddie Murphy wanted Arsenio for a starring role in *Coming to America* months prior to signing Arsenio to a managerial contract in September 1987. This would, of course, explain why Roy Gerber had been so unceremoniously dropped by Arsenio. And why the Paramount contract was also executed within days of Arsenio having signed with Wachs.

As for the million dollars, Arsenio told Cynthia

Gilbert he was going to receive . . . this was pretty close to the truth. The Paramount contract called for Arsenio to receive $100,000 for his first film and $300,000 for his second film, with all of the money to be paid to him up front. This was all in addition to the $30,000 "writing fee" he received for his contribution to the *Coming to America* script; it did not include the monies he would derive from his lucrative TV package.

The bottom line was that Arsenio would have been a fool at that point *not* to have joined forces with Wachs, who, turned him into an overnight millionaire.

So Arsenio signed with X-Management and, days later, with Paramount Studios. And because he trusted Wachs, he did not have an attorney review either of the contracts. And as Lipsky would later testify at his deposition, neither he nor Wachs suggested Arsenio do so. As Lipsky pointed out, an outside attorney reviewing the management contract might have explained the ramifications of the deal to Arsenio that Wachs, an attorney himself, had failed to explain.

The deposition testimony also revealed that Wachs had failed to explain to Arsenio that his Fox contract gave them the right to negotiate with him through June 1988, and then to prevent him from working as a late-night talk-show host until January 1989. This is, of course, why Fox had initially filed a breach of contract against Arsenio.

According to the testimony, Wachs had placed both Arsenio and Paramount in an embarrassing situation by having the studio enter into negotiations in January 1988. More important, Wachs did not reveal the contents of the Fox contract to Paramount until the studio was already negotiating for Arsenio's services. It was only then that Paramount realized it had no right to negotiate with Arsenio and, in fact, could be subject to litigation from Fox.

The studio had immediately ended the negotiations, which, according to court records, had been so "acrimonious" that Paramount at one point had terminated them. But Wachs, who had been unable to straighten out the problems with Fox, was unconcerned. He wanted to end the negotiations with Paramount anyway. It was his partner, Mark Lipsky, who apparently felt the Paramount deal would be a golden opportunity for Arsenio and reopened the discussion of Arsenio's talk show.

Thus, when June 1988 passed and Fox lost the right to negotiate with Arsenio, it was Paramount and Lipsky who began talking anew. Paramount wanted to meet with Arsenio personally at that point, and a meeting was arranged. It was only then that Arsenio learned Paramount had previously requested several meetings with him only to be told each time by Wachs that his client was not interested.

By the time Arsenio instructed his attorneys to sever his relationship with X-Management, he had become convinced that Wachs and his company were more detrimental than helpful in shaping his career.

In retaliation, X-Management's attorneys filed a countersuit in L.A. Superior Court on October 15, 1990, charging Arsenio with breach of contract and alleging that Wachs was entitled to half of all the profits from "The Arsenio Hall Show" as well as $75 million in damages for that breach of contract. In his suit, Wachs again claimed Arsenio had entered into an oral agreement in 1988 for a fifty-fifty division of profits with his company, and that this oral agreement was in addition to the standard management agreement he had signed in September 1987.

In a separate challenge, Wachs filed a suit against the California Labor Comission alleging that the State Talent Agencies Act, which he was accused of violating, was unconstitutional.

According to court documents in Wach's suit against Arsenio, the subject of the fifty-fifty split arose during an October 1989 meeting at Wach's home between Arsenio, Wachs, Lipsky, and Mark Landsman. The meeting only lasted ten minutes, however, because when Wachs told Arsenio that by an oral agreement X-Management was entitled to 50 percent of all profits from "The Arsenio Hall Show," Arsenio had called Wachs a liar, shouted that there was "no way he would be paying 50 percent and there never was such an agreement," and walked out of the meeting.

The following year in his lawsuit against Arsenio, Wachs stated that Hall had fired him and Lipsky, on August 9, 1990, to prevent them from obtaining their rightful share of the profits from "The Arsenio Hall Show." The suit also outlined the various fees Arsenio had been paid for his services, such as the $100,000 for his thirteen-week gig on the "Late Show," plus a weekly wardrobe allowance of $2,000; $430,000 for his initial two-picture deal with Paramount; and a base salary of $2.5 million a year for being the host and executive producer of his Paramount show, as well as 20 to 40 percent of that show's profits, which, in 1989, had amounted to $3 million and were expected to be $10 million in 1990.

When he had filed the suit against Arsenio, Wachs was still Eddie Murphy's manager. Only a month later, however, Eddie fired him, but retained Mark Lipsky as his personal manager. Arsenio also retained Lipsky as his financial consultant, after Lipsky disavowed any knowledge of the alleged oral contract and left X-Management shortly after Arsenio filed suit.

Originally a New York City certified public accountant, Lipsky had become the business manager in the late seventies for several members of the "Saturday Night Live" cast, including John Belushi and Dan Aykroyd. It was through his "SNL" clients that Lipsky, in April 1982, met Eddie Murphy, and a short while later had become his accountant. In turn, it was through Murphy that he met Robert Wachs and became his accountant, too.

Five years later, in January 1987, Lipsky joined Wachs and became a stockholder in Eddie Murphy Productions as well as Eddie Murphy Television. In doing so, he became one of Murphy's personal managers and, of course, became one of Arsenio's managers that same year. The rest, as the cliché goes, is history, all of which is documented in the records of Los Angeles Superior Court.

Unlike his behavior during his feud with Willis Edwards the year before, Arsenio kept his mouth shut this time. "No comment" was all the press could get out of him and his minions until the suit was settled.

The Wachs suit hung over Arsenio's head until April 1992, when, in a surprising victory, the California Labor Commission ordered X-Management to return the $2 million in commissions they had collected from August 9, 1989, to August 8, 1990, to Hall. The commission agreed with Arsenio's attorneys that since X-Management was not a licensed talent agency, the company had acted improperly in procuring employment for him.

On May 5, 1992, however, attorneys for X-Management filed an appeal with the State Labor Commission and that case is still pending. On February 17, 1993, Wachs' separate suit alleging that the Talent Agencies Act was unconstitutional was rejected by the California Court of Appeals.

"It was the most painful thing that ever happened to me," Arsenio recently confessed. "It's the only time the people I work with have seen me break down and cry like a baby. When I found out all the realities of the testimony, found out during the trial that everyone in my life had been trying to fuck me and take my money, I was in pain. I was buckled up, man."

According to Arsenio, he hadn't had an attorney read over the management agreement he had signed with Wachs in 1987 because he trusted Wachs, who, he said, had always told him "You're like a son to me, and I would never do anything to hurt you."

"Basically," Arsenio admitted, "I was an idiot. I trusted him on a lot of things. Now, because of what I found out during the trial, I've taken over all power of attorney. Nobody can buy Tabasco sauce without my signature. Nobody gets any power over anything, because I have seen what they will do if they can.

"So," he concluded, "the bottom line is I don't trust anybody now. I let them administer my life, but I took any right of power of attorney away from them. And if I see anybody remove a toenail off my carpet, they're gonna be gone!"

Although there was trouble below the surface in the spring of 1990, everything appeared to be in tip top shape. The talk show was comfortably ensconced in the ratings, and everyone was excited about an upcoming appearance by Madonna, the shock-turned-to-schlock girl, who had chosen Arsenio's show for her only TV talk-show exposure of the year.

Having Madonna as a guest in May 1990 was such a coup that Arsenio and his producer, Marla Kell Brown, decided to devote more than half of the hourlong show to her musings. Little did they realize, however, just what her musings would be.

No sooner had the blond bombshell taken her place on Arsenio's couch than a bawdy night of often-bleeped barbs began. By the time it ended forty-five minutes later, what had begun in jest had deteriorated into an unflattering exercise one-upmanship between the two mighty mouths.

An audible gasp from the studio audience could be heard when Madonna, after teasing him about his relationship with Paula Abdul, coyly suggested that she had heard a rumor that Arsenio and Eddie Murphy were lovers.

Another gasp followed when Arsenio, without missing a beat, rebounded with a sarcastic comment about her supposed lesbian relationship with comedienne Sandra Bernhard.

MADONNA: What about Eddie Murphy?
ARSENIO: Did I pull his tights down, too?
MADONNA: I heard that you did . . . now, seriously, there is a rumor, and I want to know about it.
ARSENIO: Well, there's a rumor about you and Sandra Bernhard, but I didn't ask you. . . .
MADONNA: What do you want to know? I've never pulled her tights down. . . .
ARSENIO: She probably arrived at your house already naked.

Although Arsenio played it cool on the air, he went into a backstage rage after the taping. "Was she on something, or did she go crazy?" he yelled. "I put my whole life into that show and that bitch embarrassed me in front of seven million people."

Madonna, who left the studio as soon as her segment was finished and was on a plane headed to Houston by the time Arsenio had his tantrum, supposedly was equally unhappy with her host. "He has a large following, which is why I did the show to begin with. But he's really mean-spirited," she reportedly told a friend. "I'll never do his show again. I don't need that kind of abuse."

The show was an absolute ratings hit, giving Arsenio the largest audience in the history of his show and beating out "the Tonight Show."

Publicly the feud was played down. "Arsenio loved it," Marla Kell Brown, Arsenio's producer and head "angel," told inquiring minds from the nation's press. "He told me today if he could have her back on the show tonight, he would. For Arsenio, it's his perfect kind of show—unpredictable and spontaneous.

"Sometimes when you book a big name and you build it up, you worry if they'll live up to everyone's expectations. But she surpassed them," Brown concluded. "We just had a lot of laughs."

Two weeks after the Madonna incident Arsenio told a *USA Today* writer, "If Madonna stops enjoying herself, then I'm an ass. If Arsenio is the victim, it's good TV. What you've got to remember about Madonna is that this is just fun and games."

But only a month later Arsenio lashed out at the Material Girl, admitting he was angry about her description of his haircut as "tired" and her comment that "if you were one of my dancers, you couldn't wear your hair like that."

"I had a devil sitting on one shoulder saying, 'Crush this girl's world,' Arsenio told *TV Guide* in mid-June. And I could have done it. I'm a stand-up comic. I deal with hecklers for a living. I've made people cry and run out of a club after heckling me. I know I can go off," he concluded. "I'm from the clubs, I'm from the smoke and the dope. I'm from the g-h-e-t-t-o."

Not long after this, he gave an *Ebony* magazine writer a message for Madonna. "First, Madonna, I will never have to work for you because I have as much money as you have. Number two, I've seen your dancers and . . . I'm nothing like them. They work FOR you. I work WITH you. Point number three is you wanted to be black when you were little but you are not black, so don't try to understand blackness. It is not your place to dictate black hair care or fashion. You have borrowed our sound but not our sensibilities, so don't make an attempt to tell me how I should look."

Two years later, in June 1992, all apparently was forgiven because the Material Girl paid Arsenio a second visit. Compared with the first, this one was low-key. However, it did earn Arsenio one of his all-time highest ratings, allowing him to top "the post-Carson Tonight Show."

If Arsenio was overreacting to Madonna's criticism of his hairstyle, it was probably because he had endured a "hair attack" earlier that year from LaToya Jackson, who had taken exception to his comments about her breasts having been surgically enlarged in a tongue-in-cheek but pointed letter.

"Dear Arsenio," the letter began, "I have to get

something off my chest. I am very disappointed that you have continued making ridiculous and untrue statements claiming that my breasts have been artificially enlarged. If you 'feel' you are qualified to tell the difference, you are quite welcome to visit me the next time you're in New York."

Arsenio being Arsenio, he read the letter on the air. And promptly received a second letter, along with a waffle iron and ten pounds of hairstyling gel. "Knowing how meticulous you are about your appearance and the amount of time you spend on your hair each day, I tried to select items that would make this process quicker and easier," read the accompanying note.

Yet a third note arrived, accompanied with an electric razor. "Dear Arsenio," LaToya penned, "why don't you try just shaving your head and starting over again."

By the beginning of the following season, Arsenio had changed his hairstyle but, he declared, it had nothing to do with Madonna or LaToya. He said he had simply wanted something different from his squared-off, hip-hop style of 1990. So when Scott Julian, an Atlanta stylist, sent him a letter and sketch of what *he* would do with Arsenio's hair, the talk-show host gave him the go-ahead.

"I told him let's do it for the MTV Awards so I can be criticized internationally," Arsenio laughed, adding, "In the ghetto, it would be termed fried, dyed, and kicked to the side."

But in 1990 not even a new hair style would have helped. Arsenio, it seemed, was under attack from everyone about everything that year. His most public feud of the year was not with Madonna or LaToya but was with none other than Roseanne Arnold, who took loud offense to his ongoing series of fat jokes aimed directly at her.

"I thought I could do Roseanne jokes because I went to see Roseanne and Louie Anderson once at the Universal Amphitheater and they both did fat jokes," Arsenio would later explain.

"So my thing was—and this might be a naive point of view—she does this kind of stuff, so she's probably cool with it. Like, if you see me come on the air and say, 'Hey, look, I don't know why the women are screaming. I have little tiny ears. I don't know what they see sexy.' Then somebody's going to say, 'He jokes about his ears. So why can't I do a joke about his ears?' These ears should not even be on my head. Really, I'm serious."

The feud, which ended in late 1990, had actually begun in late 1989, not long after the release of Roseanne's autobiography, *My Life As a Woman*. "A lot of people will see her face on this book and be mad when they find out there ain't no recipes inside," Arsenio had joked on the show. "It's not a cookbook." Another time, talking about their ongoing feud, Arsenio told his audience, "It's not over until Roseanne sings."

"*A Pocketful of Miracle Whip* should be the title of her next book," Arsenio joked during another edition of his show. "The book tells that her father was a slob. That's what interests me. When you look at Roseanne, you would never know, huh?"

"I'd like to slap him two ways," Roseanne told Oprah Winfrey during an October 1989 interview. "His head is a triangle. He parts it so it even looks more like a triangle."

Then, growing serious, Roseanne told Oprah, "I don't think Arsenio's jokes are funny. The jokes are saying that certain women who are bigger than others don't look right. I never hear any fat-guy jokes. I think these jokes are right in there with racist jokes and ethnic jokes, because they have a victim. They're jokes most of us have grown past. I think they're racist."

Arsenio disagreed. "No, I don't buy that," he told several reporters. "Fat people weren't brought from fatland and forced to work free and separated from their fat relatives and hung from large trees."

If there had been bad blood between the two prior to the comedienne's marriage to Tom Arnold, however, Roseanne's blood really began to boil when Arsenio showed his TV audience an aerial photo of Tom and Roseanne lolling around a swimming pool in bathing suits during their honeymoon. "Remember the whales?" he laughing asked the audience while flashing the photos in front of the camera. "Well, they're back."

The battle turned verbally ugly when Roseanne, not noted for recognizing the boundaries of good taste herself, retaliated by telling her audience "There have been a lotta great comedy teams in the world: Lucy and Ricky, George and Gracie, and Arsenio and Jim Nabors."

Roseanne's jab about Arsenio came less than a year after rumors had circulated throughout Hollywood concerning Arsenio's relationship with Eddie Murphy and with boxing champion Mike Tyson.

Although he made light of the accusations, Arsenio was both concerned and hurt by them, which is why he was actually pleased when a reporter called him up, asking about his relationship with Paula Abdul. "I got a call from one of the tabloid's and they said, 'We saw you coming out of Paula Abdul's house at five in the morning.' I said 'So? So now you know that you won't see me coming out of some guy's house. I'm a normal, healthy American talk-show host.'"

Not long after, while in the midst of a *TV Guide* interview, Arsenio suddenly brought up the rumor concerning his relationship with Mike Tyson with a writer from the magazine.

"See, Mike was hanging out on the set quite a bit for a while and a rumor was going around the lot that he was interested in a girl around here," Arsenio began, switching topics almost in mid-sentence. "But there was another rumor, that Mike Tyson and I were lovers and the girl just a front.

"When you're in bed at night, that hurts. People sayin' you're homosexual and you're not, that's nasty," Arsenio confided to the stunned reporter, who dutifully recorded his anguish.

And not long after that, Arsenio, no wimp in the insult arena himself, took off the gloves and squared off against Roseanne.

"Jim Nabors? Hmmmm . . . ," Arsenio retorted. "I'd still make out better than Tom Arnold did."

"My thing is, if you do a joke on my show and call me gay, what's the rule," he would later say. "When you challenge a black man's manhood, there are no rules anymore."

Thus, Arsenio continued to poke fun at Roseanne, even taking a jab at her sex life with Tom Arnold. "It's like a new ride," he told his studio audience. "Magic Mountain. It's a wild ride, but it's nothing like the ride Tom Arnold takes every night."

In June, 1990, Roseanne took her act on the road, devoting the last three minutes of her show to Arsenio. "It isn't often we get to see a black nerd; most nerds are white," she told her SRO crowd in the Vegas Hilton showroom. She followed this by calling Arsenio a "triangle-headed Eddie Murphy look-alike."

She repeated the same material a month later during a performance at Trump Castle in Atlantic City, only a couple of weeks after Tom Arnold had showed up at Paramount Studios unannounced with a full camera crew, hoping to crash Arsenio's show. After the security guards wouldn't allow him on the lot, Arnold waited outside, hoping to get Arsenio when he drove off the lot. However, Arsenio exited in a limo and apparently didn't know Arnold was even present until the following day.

Realizing he had started the feud and, therefore, it was up to him to end the public bickering, Arsenio telephoned Tom Arnold and told him he realized he was really hurting Roseanne with the jokes. "She said the photograph had invaded her privacy, which is true," Arsenio later admitted. "And I further invaded it by showing the pictures on the air. I became a little sensitive to what she said and felt that maybe I was a jerk. So I stopped."

In an attempt at reconciliation, Arsenio invited Tom and Roseanne to be guests on his show, and they accepted. The threesome appeared together in mid-November 1990, and Roseanne admitted she had been hurt by Arsenio's jokes about her shape. "It's only when you talk about my boobs and stuff," she confessed. "I can take fat jokes, but you're not funny."

"But you called me Triangle Head," Arsenio pointed out, "and you know I'm sensitive about the shape of my head."

Roseanne simply looked at him and smiled.

By the end of 1990, Arsenio was smiling, too. Despite the feuds, the lawsuits, and the bizarre threats, 1990 had turned out to be a better-than-all-right twelve months. It was the "Year of Arsenio Hall," the year that Arsenio's childhood dream of having his own star on the Hollywood Walk of Fame became a reality.

With his mother, Annie, proudly at his side, and his then-good-friend Jay Leno standing nearby, Arsenio became the 1,923rd entertainer to get a star bearing his name on the Hollywood Walk of Fame, right next to that of the legendary Marilyn Monroe and only a few steps from McDonald's. The date was November 16, 1990, and it is unlikely Arsenio will ever forget it.

It was a dream come true, one more childhood fantasy he could check off of his dwindling wish list. Arsenio Hall had left the Cleveland ghetto of his childhood far behind. He had become a symbol of the American Dream attained.

By the time Arsenio knelt beside his Walk of Fame star only a week before Thanksgiving, he had become a powerful force at Paramount Studios, which, in April, had rewarded his contribution to the company coffers by turning the old Gloria Swanson Building into the Arsenio Hall Communications Building. And to make certain that everyone knew just whose offices were housed in the two-story stucco quarters, the studio had installed a large, prominently placed plaque heralding ARSENIO HALL COMMUNICATIONS, LTD. beside the building's entrance.

"Arsenio needs a bigger office for his swelled head," actor Woody Harrelson supposedly had fumed after being asked by Paramount to vacate his office to make more room for Arsenio, who was already encamped in Bing Crosby's former digs. But Woody *did* move to another office.

Adding to Arsenio's new luster was his selection in June 1990 as "Television Personality of the Year" by TV GUIDE and also "Entertainer of the Year" in an

US magazine reader poll. By that time he had already won the Sammy Davis, Jr., Award at the Fourth Annual Soul Train Music Awards ceremony on March 14, 1990, and had earned the People's Choice Award as "Favorite Late Night Talk Show Host."

"The bottom line is," Arsenio had joked, referring to the People's Choice Award, "that they can't say my relatives voted for me. They have to accept that this black man is doing it not in his own private arena, not in the ghetto of Cleveland, but in their arena . . . They can no longer put us in the Negro League. We are bad in any color of the rainbow."

With all of the kudos and Paramount cash being lavished upon him, it's no wonder that in a moment of exuberance Arsenio declared, "Every day is this incredible joyride through life."

Arsenio's joyride hit a bumpy road, however, when Keenen Wayans began delivering biting parodies of him on "In Living Color," shortly after the popular Fox comedy series made its April 15, 1990, debut.

Not that Wayans didn't give Arsenio fair warning. "Arsenio's just ripe for parody," Wayans had told several writers. "He's easy to do because he has so many Arsenio-isms, like his laugh, what he does with his hands during interviews, and how he blanks out on his guests.

"Sometimes, while he's interviewing people, you can see in his eyes that he's thinking about hanging out after the show. There's also no expounding on profound thoughts. He once had Angela Davis, the sixties radical, on the show, and she was going on about communism, capitalism and the meaning of the sixties, and at the end Arsenio just said, 'Yeah. We'll be right back.' Larry King he's not."

Thus, shortly after "Color" premiered, Wayans, portraying Arsenio, and David Alan Grier, playing Marion Barry, the impeached mayor of Washington, D.C., appeared in a send-up of Arsenio's much-discussed obsequious interview techniques. Wearing padded buttocks, constantly dropping Eddie Murphy's name, and fawning over his guest, Wayans paid devastating homage to Arsenio's oft-criticized on-camera style.

> ARSENIO/WAYANS: *My people tell me you've written a book.* . . .
> BARRY/CRIER: *I didn't write a book. I WAS booked!*

As Arsenio, Wayans then showed a clip of Barry's supposed "new movie," which turned out to be a videotape of his arrest in a D.C. hotel room.

Arsenio vehemently denied the published reports of a subsequent rift between him and Wayans, explaining, "I didn't take offense at all. I told Keenen, when we met at a barbecue at Eddie's a couple of days later, that not only did I laugh, but we showed it at a morning meeting here for everybody. Not only do I not think the skit was mean-spirited . . . there was a part in it they took out that I thought was hilarious and should have been kept in." (The edited part to which Arsenio was referring involved Wayans having "Hello, Eddie" stenciled on the soles of his shoes and continually raising his feet to the camera in an obvious jab at Arsenio's constant references to his friendship with Eddie Murphy.)

"It's flattering," Arsenio was telling the press in October 1990. "They do Michael Jackson one week, they do Mike Tyson, they do me. What that says is that 'Yo, man, you are large!' To be parodied, there has to be an understanding that everyone knows who this guy is. You know when "Saturday Night Live" did Arsenio Beckman, that was some funny shit. How can you not laugh at it? Rob Lowe played Arsenio Beckman and he had these extra-long fingertips. First you look and you say, 'I'm going to kill Rob!' And then you find yourself saying, "Yo! This is the price of fame.' When you're large, part of it is being ridiculed and dogged."

Months later, however, Arsenio felt compelled to explain that he and Wayans had never really been close, contradicting the recollections of everyone who knew both men in the early eighties.

"There are so many misperceptions in this business," Arsenio explained. "One of them is that Keenen and I used to be big buddies. We were trying to get him on the show, but usually I don't even see him. I don't really hang with most comics."

In light of his past membership in so-called the Black Pack and the fact that Eddie Murphy had originally met Arsenio through Keenen when Wayans was writing for him in the early eighties, Arsenio's comment about the friendship must have come as something of a surprise to Keenen.

Whatever his private response, publicly Wayans simply shrugged off the loss. "Most celebrities are flattered by the satires," he said. "They're excited about someone doing them because they don't get impersonated that often. Even when brutal, if it's funny, they can accept it.

"I don't know why Arsenio wouldn't put me on his show," he added. "He never gave me a reason. All I know is that one day I found out my friend wasn't my friend anymore."

The answer is, of course, that despite his public denials, Arsenio was hurt and embarrassed by the sketch, not because of the parody of his interviewing techniques but because he is super sensitive about having a large rear end, even though he has joked about it himself in the past. It was Wayans's use of the padded butt that created the rift and Wayans quickly found his name had been banned from Arsenio's guest list.

The truth is that behind Arsenio's finely honed aura of Muhammad Ali–like confidence and his frequent moments of jaw-jutting belligerence, there lies an extremely insecure man.

This was never more obvious than in September 1989 when Arsenio had worried aloud about whether or not he had become "a joke." "I notice on other shows now, like Letterman, you see Dave and Paul Shaffer doing jokes about me," he had confided to an interviewer. "And Dennis Miller said something one night [on "Saturday Night Live"] when people were laughing and applauding him, like, 'Stop it, stop it. You're going to make me think I'm Arsenio Hall or something.' And they laughed even more.

"When you're quiet, in a room alone, you start thinking, 'Why were they clapping? Am I a joke or something to them?'"

"What I'm trying to say," he finally admitted, "is that I don't want to turn into some joke. It makes me very cautious."

Despite these moments of doubt, though, by the end of 1990, Arsenio's ego had become so inflated, his vision of himself so grandiose, that he didn't need "In Living Color" to parody him. He had become a parody of himself. In a classic case of too much too soon, Mr. Humble had become an unattractive portrait of pomposity. It is a portrait that, unfortunately, has not faded with the passing of time. If anything, it's become even more vivid.

CHAPTER

9

"**My woman is show business,**" **Arsenio has** often said, explaining his bachelorhood. "I don't know how anybody who is successful has a family life. Sometimes I say to myself, 'You're thirty-six. There should be something that looks like you running around the house and a woman who's saying 'Dear, Irving Azoff's on the phone.'

"But my life is in front of people. So when I go home, I don't want to hear voices. There's nobody in my house that'll tell me I can't make it, because there ain't nobody there. I'm alone," he said, "and I'm happy being alone. That's how you insulate yourself from negativity."

Thus, in lieu of a wife and, if you choose to believe him, a life, Arsenio prefers to spend most of his time with his self-professed mistress: "The Arsenio Hall Show."

The cavernous Stage 29 is his nightly love nest, where he coddles and coos at people across the country. And his second-floor office, overlooking Gower Street in the heart of Hollywood, is where he really lives.

Safeguarded from an often-cruel world by a bullet-proof glass door and a receptionist, whose job of answering the phone is secondary to making sure her boss is securely protected from intruders, Arsenio's office is accessible only by key or the push of a hidden button activating the electronic door lock.

Once inside the hallowed corridors, visitors can usually find Arsenio sitting in a black leather swivel chair behind an immense black marble half-moon desk in an office roughly the size of a small racquetball court. Although the office is large and could be airy, with its large windows facing west, Arsenio prefers to keep the blinds drawn, shutting out both the Southern California sun and the sound of city traffic on Gower Street. As a result the office usually resembles a dark lair, a testament to Arsenio's night-owl life-style.

It is here, with Marla Kell Brown's office directly across the hall and that of his secretary just next door, that Arsenio feels the most secure. It is while sitting behind his shiny black fifteen-foot horseshoe-shaped desk that he feels the most powerful, perhaps even omnipotent on a particularly good day.

Usually topped by a bowl of popcorn as well as stacks of papers, the desk dominates the black-and-gray high-tech office. "When I first got this office, it seemed so big. It was like there was an echo in here," Arsenio said. "Now the echo has started to disappear. The walls are starting to close in. This place isn't so big anymore and I like things big.

"In fact," Arsenio joked, "when I die, I want a huge casket that I can roll around in and dial '9' to get out from."

Several bookcases, holding an eclectic assortment of books, electronic toys, mementos, and CDs, line the office walls. One of them is devoted almost solely to Arsenio's complete collection of original episodes from "The Fugitive," the David Janssen ABC series of yesteryear. "If I could drive and watch TV without killing myself, I would," Arsenio has often joked. "I'm addicted to television."

A synthesizer and a huge black drum set occupy a corner of the office. The drum set is the realization of a promise Arsenio made to himself as a child when, sorely in need of money, Annie Hall was forced to sell his original drum set. Watching the drum set leave the house, Arsenio had promised himself that when he made it, he'd buy a new set. He fulfilled that promise in July 1989.

The office is filled with photographs of Arsenio's celebrity friends. At one point, the largest portrait in his ever-increasing collection was of his early mentor Nancy Wilson. "I don't know where I'd be without her," Arsenio has often told guests. "The Midwest somewhere. Probably Cleveland."

Other photographs gracing the walls and the book-shelves are of pals Eddie Murphy, Magic Johnson, and Patti LaBelle, as well as his idol Johnny Carson. Most of all, however, there are photos of Arsenio. Arsenio alone. Arsenio with friends. Arsenio with guests. Arsenio magazine covers. Arsenio advertisements. Arsenio posters. Only a blind person could not know this is the power base of Arsenio Hall.

With its large oversized neon sculpture of his now famous signature, the immense collection of stuffed animals, the plastic basketball hoop hanging from the ceiling, the large TV monitor also hanging from the ceiling, the office is a perfect reflection of the life, times, and interests of Arsenio Hall.

"I live here. Everything I have at home is also

here and this office," he says of the dimly lighted lair. "I spend more time here than I do at home. I'm happier when I'm working than when I'm not." Which is why, he explains, "When I go home, I take my briefcase, sit it on my desk, turn on the TV, and assume the exact same situation. Sometimes when people force me to articulate what I do, I realize that I'm this entertainment and show-biz machine, and clearly I should go out and purchase a life."

"I think, if anything, Arsenio has become more reclusive because of the extent of his celebrity," Marla Kell Brown explained in a 1991 interview. "He can't go anywhere without being recognized, which is difficult for him, because he likes to be just a guy. He likes to go the gym and just play. He likes to go to a basketball game and just watch the game like the other guys. But it's almost impossible.

"He has more of a personal social life on the weekends," she continued, "and he's become less of a hermit since he started the show. He's more comfortable, more confident walking into a restaurant and he does seem to go out more, but he's not a big partier, although people think he is," concluded Arsenio's chief protector.

In contrast to his office, Arsenio's dressing room is a tiny cubicle. It is here that he prepares himself for his nightly escapades as host of a syndicated show. It is here, seated in a tall director's chair, surrounded by a hairstylist who goes to great lengths to cover up fact that his hair is beginning to thin, and a makeup girl, that Arsenio confers with Kell Brown and the other show execs, going over last-minute details, such as the opening-monologue cue cards, shortly before the show's 5:15 P.M. taping.

The dressing room, which has a giant theatrical

mirror covering an entire half of one wall, also consists of a mini-bathroom, shower, and wardrobe closet plus a well-stocked bar, whence Arsenio always pours himself at least one shot of Jack Daniel's just prior to taping the show.

It is here, in the environs of Arsenio Hall Communications, Ltd., surrounded by "Arsenio's Angels," as he has dubbed his mostly female staff, that Arsenio appears to be happiest. And why not? He is protected, pampered, nurtured, and revered from the moment he arrives at his second-floor office around 11:00 A.M. until he departs roughly nine hours later. And if that isn't enough, five nights a week he spends an hour in front of a capacity crowd on Stage 29, where adoring public barks their approval and gives the old Arsenio wrist-twisting, arm-turning seal of approval.

Women, young or old, relatives or employees, have always provided a safe harbor for Arsenio, a fact he readily acknowledges. "My sensibilities, my choices, my approach to life all have a slight twist that's been formulated by these ladies. Men are men. Men start wars. Men are different," he explained. "But the things these women bring and give to me mentally sends me out on the air. The women in my life today, just like those women who raised me, keep me straight."

In return for this supposed "straight" thinking, Arsenio does not tolerate mistreatment of his female staffers by anyone, including celebrity guests, one of whom was forever banished from the show because he "grabbed somebody's rear end." There also was an employee who was forced to resign after he repeatedly harassed several of the women.

"There's a comfort zone for Arsenio with women,"

Kell Brown once explained. "He was raised by women and has always been around women, but I also think women talk things out differently. Egos are different for the most part with women.

"Arsenio is a very talkative, sensitive, reflective person, and he often talks in feelings," she added. "We have conversations. We have exchanges. We don't get into ego plays—and I think Arsenio is probably more comfortable with that," she concluded.

Cheryl Bonacci, the twenty-seven-year-old vice-president of Arsenio Hall Communications, echoed Kell Brown's sentiments. "Arsenio's a sensitive, emotional, and creative person," she said. "I don't know if those are traits you would find more often in women, but that's the way he was raised, and those are the sensibilities he acquired.

"There are a lot of people who want to be around Arsenio and just make him happy and impress him so much that they'll do anything," Bonacci concluded. "They just keep putting him on a pedestal, which is not what he wants; he just wants you to be real."

An interesting footnote to Bonacci's comments about her boss is that in early 1991, while Arsenio was playing man about town, she and the A-Man were reported by the nation's tabloids to be lovers, quietly living together in Arsenio's Studio City home. The story of their relationship apparently began after Cheryl, a pretty brunette, was promoted in May 1990 from Arsenio's secretary to a vice-presidency of Arsenio Hall Communications, Inc., quite a leap even for the most imaginative mind.

In truth, by the time the relationship had been discovered by the tabloids, it was already on the wane, if not over, having actually begun when Arsenio was hosting the Fox network's "Late Show." At that point, Cheryl Bonacci had been merely a young, poorly paid production assistant. It was then, according to several former "Late Show" staffers, including one who accidentally discovered the two of them together in a compromising position, that Cheryl took her first step forward in what had otherwise been a lackluster career.

The affair between Arsenio and Cheryl was only one of many rumored liaisons involving Arsenio and his female staffers. In December 1989, he was reported to be romantically involved with his twenty-four-year-old publicist, Dana Freedman, who subsequently left her job at the Bender, Goldman, Helper public-relations agency and joined Arsenio's staff as his spokesperson, taking the account with her, of course.

Since then there have been numerous stories of flings between Arsenio and at least three other female staffers, all of whom are still with the show, working in wondrous peace and apparent harmony with each other. (Dana Freedman, however, departed the Hall show, where she had been vice-president of marketing since 1992, in early 1993 to join 20th Century Fox as vice-president of publicity for the studio's television division.)

"I'm not surprised to hear that," confided a close friend of Arsenio's from the mid-eighties. "He was always chasing women and he almost always caught them. Women love Arsenio because he plays that helpless, little-boy routine. He's very manipulative.

"Truthfully I've never known him NOT to have at least one woman in his life, and usually it's been more than one. Most of them have been white women, too, although I've known him to date several pretty black women. At one point several years ago, he was dating a beautiful Puerto Rican gal. All that stuff he gives out about being alone so much and liking it? It's just bullshit."

As for Arsenio, he is neither admitting nor denying anything involving his "angels," other than to concede, "I like women younger than me. It helps keep me young."

If there is an "angel" second to Marla Kell Brown, especially in the area of flattery, it has to be Arsenio's director, Sandi Fullerton, who believes Arsenio is "a lot more brilliant than you see on camera. He pushes you hard," she admitted, "but not as hard as he pushes himself."

Adding her voice to the angelic chorus of his supporters is the ever-present, insightful Kell Brown, with whom he purportedly spends hours on the phone. "There's a real modest, humble side to Arsenio," Kell Brown once said. "There's a fine line between confidence and cocky. Look at great athletes—they go in with confidence. I see Arsenio as a confident host, but someone who is also a student. If he had nothing to learn, we wouldn't be spending all of these hours on the phone."

Young, female, white, and from suburban Chicago, Kell Brown appears to be a perfect foil for Arsenio and his black urban Cleveland background. "We trust each other's feelings," she has said. "If Arsenio and I were the same type of person, it wouldn't work." Of all the women on Arsenio's staff, Kell Brown appears to be the one most protective of her boss. She also appeared to be the one person who could rein in the exuberant Arsenio when he became too effusive, or got carried away with his now notorious raunchy asides or naughty flirtations with his female guests.

"He can push the boundaries because of his

schoolboy charm and mischievous wit," Brown conceded. "That's when he's at his best, when he's as close to the line as possible. However, if he pushes the boundaries too far one night, we kind of look at each other and say, 'We went a little far,' and then, for the next few nights at least, he'll be on his best behavior."

It is these excesses that have shaped the show and, at the same time, have led to numerous criticisms of Hall's interviewing technique. The latter, characterized by warmth and humor and an intimacy that has Hall seated quite close to his guests, had led some TV critics to wonder whether or not the night will come when a guest will actually jump in his lap. So far both Arsenio and his viewers have been spared that experience, with the notable exception of Whitney Houston, who sat in his lap during a giddy conversation between guests Eddie Murphy and Sheena Easton and their host.

Another criticism of Arsenio, one that hounds him to this day, is that he is not a good interviewer. "His treatment of guests is overly deferential, his questions stultifying softballs," penned Richard Zoglin, *Time* magazine's esteemed television critic, in a November 1989 cover story. "Hall seems tied to preset questions and often appears disconnected and unresponsive. Too many comments elicit a blank 'mmmm-hmmmm,' followed by an awkward silence."

Apparently the Paramount TV executives agreed because, only months after he went on the air, the studio suggested Arsenio undertake several weeks of intensive coaching from Virginia Sherwood, a New York–based media consultant, who urged him to ask more follow-up questions and avoid overusing words like interesting. It was one of the few times

Arsenio, even begrudgingly, took the studio's advice.

"It was very overwhelming when I started. I had on a lot of hats. I would be sitting, talking to somebody, and would look over and wonder what was wrong with a camera," Arsenio explained, adding, "Or I'd hear a scuffle and wonder what was going on. I would think a segment was running too long and wonder about a timing cue. I'd look over at Michael {Wolff} and wonder whether his headset was off.

"Whatever was going on," he continued, "I had to learn that for that hour I had to take the other hats off and focus on the conversation, that I'd better listen like nothing else existed." But listening is not a comedian's forte. No one knows that better than Arsenio.

"Comics generally don't listen," Arsenio conceded. "We're used to saying, 'This is my show.' Our biggest problem is that we're on stage all the time. We're selfish. We're our own writers. We're unable to listen and share because we're too busy fighting for laughs.

"I've heard people in the audience say something complimentary to a comic, and he thinks he's being heckled," he continued. Comedians are individuals, but a good talk-show host only gets a laugh when the show needs it. When there's a dip or a void, that's when the comic should rush in. You have to remember that the audience has tuned into see the guest. You're there all the time.

"What makes Johnny Carson so great," he added, "is that he's not an overpowering stand-up comic. He has an incredible understanding of when he's needed and when he's not. He'll insert comedy when there's a bad guest and stay out of Robin Williams's way. Doing a talk show for him is like a snooze alarm on a clock. He can find it in the dark. He doesn't care about numbers or competitors. It's like Tyson: nobody can beat him."

The constant criticisms of the press forced Arsenio into having to do some real soul-searching about his strengths and weaknesses. He had to look at himself with cool objectivity and then decide precisely what tack he would take an the interviewer.

"I realized that I had to decide who I wanted to please," he would later explain. "I'm a comedian. I'm not Ted Koppel. People seem to like that I don't have a malicious side. I'm a comic, and I'm trying to create a positive, informative, laugh-filled atmosphere."

As a result of Arsenio's "positive atmosphere," he has been branded an insipid, fawning modern-day Merv Griffin. It's a criticism he has heard, but chooses to overlook. "Yeah," he conceded, "that stuff used to bother me. Then I thought, 'Arsenio, you're more famous than this guy writing about you.'

"I have to dance with the girl I brought. I'm this guy, and I can't be all things to all people," he explained. "So, who should I do my show for? This guy or that guy? No matter what I do, there will be criticism. I can't please everybody, so I've decided to simply please myself and do the best job I can. If I did it any other way, I'd be an inconsistent, confusing retard on the air."

A typical day begins with Arsenio, who's usually up by 9:00 A.M., arriving at the office around 11:00 A.M. to meet with his various executives and discuss the day's show, projects in development, and marketing strategies. By 2:00 P.M., Arsenio is on Stage 29 talking with Kell Brown, Sandi Fullerton, and the show's writers, among which there has been a tremendous turnover. "He doesn't have one original staff member since the show went on the air," confided a former Paramount executive.

Although his chief rival, Jay Leno, almost always personally greets his "Tonight Show" guests, it is extremely rare for Arsenio to mix with his guests. The official reason given is that it would cut down on the spontaneity their meeting on the air. Several former Hall associates, however, claim, "The truth is that Arsenio thinks he's king and that his guests are lucky to be on his couch." So unless a guest happens to be a personal friend, like Whitney Houston or her hubby, Bobbie Brown, Sinbad, Magic Johnson, Eddie Murphy, or Patti LaBelle, chances are they will not even catch a glimpse of Arsenio until the camera is rolling.

After the hour taping, Arsenio usually goes up to his dressing room for a postmortem of the just-taped show with Kell Brown, publicist Dana Freedman, and other show execs. After that, Arsenio and Kell Brown segue to her office, where they review the night's monologue. If Arsenio's had a particularly big star on the show that night, and he believes the interview went well, he'll look at it, explained a former Hall intimate. If not, he leaves. Sometimes he goes directly home, sometimes he goes out to one of his favorite haunts, like the Roxbury Club, the trendy Sunset Boulevard eatery cum nightclub or Nicky Blair's, another industry hangout on Sunset Boulevard.

Once home, however, Arsenio customarily watches tapes of Leno and Letterman before falling asleep, usually around 2:00 A.M. and usually with a talk-radio station droning in the background. "I can't go to sleep without it," he has confessed.

Since "The Arsenio Hall Show" is one of the cornerstones upon which Paramount TV syndication is constructed, Arsenio's clout does not end at the door of his office complex. Take the time Eddie Murphy was given a golf cart to drive around Paramount, surveying his movie kingdom. Arsenio quickly requested and got one, too. Now the two of them, the King of Comedy and the Prince of Late Night, can survey their Paramount realms in tandem at five miles per hour.

Arsenio also managed to wrangle three parking spaces for his car on the Paramount lot, which is so crowded the entire neighborhood within a two-block area is overflowing with illegally parked cars. But Paramount execs understood when Arsenio explained he needed three spaces—one for his car and one on either side of his car for protection against nicks and dents.

It was, in fact, Arsenio's parking place that reportedly led to a loud, nasty brouhaha between Arsenio and a studio security guard, Shirley Ruiz, a thirty-year-old mother of four young children. When it was over, Ruiz found herself out of a job, only because she just happened to be in the wrong place on the wrong day. It is one of several unpleasant stories that have made the rounds on the Paramount lot during the last couple of years.

It was a typical Los Angeles day when Arsenio pulled onto the Paramount lot on August 20, 1990, and, for some unexplained reason, wanted to park his Porsche closer to his office than his three officially assigned spaces. Unfortunately another car was parked in that day's spot of his choice.

Angry at the intrusion of another poacher, Arsenio spied Ms. Ruiz passing by and reportedly began yelling at her about someone being parked in the spot. "He was screaming at me that he pays rent at the studio, and he told me, 'You'll do whatever I want this second,'" Ms. Ruiz would later recall for reporters.

"He spewed ugly, four-letter words and was vulgar, and kept verbally assaulting me for five minutes. People had come out of the nearby stages to see what all the shouting about," she explained.

"It was awful. His eyes were flashing wildly and his veins were popping out of his neck. I really feared for my life. I thought he was going to beat me to a pulp."

As the crowd of onlookers grew Arsenio screamed "You're stupid . . . you're fat . . . you're a pig. Do you hear me? I want this car towed out of my parking space."

Ruiz was so shocked she remembers very little of what happened afterward, other than that she was treated for an "anxiety reaction" at the nearby Kaiser Medical Center and then was taken home by her husband.

Returning to work several days later, Ruiz discovered that Arsenio had gone to the security department and had them remove her. According to Ruiz, who at that point had been employed at Paramount for two years preceding, the talk-show host refused to apologize, saying she had "a bad attitude."

Ruiz was not the only Paramount employee to fall victim to Arsenio's tirades. Not long before his encounter with her, Arsenio had a loud, angry disagreement with Milt Hoffman, Paramount's executive in charge of production. According to a former staff member, the two could be heard in the corridor, through the closed door of Arsenio's office.

At one point, confided the staff member, you could even hear a crash and the sound of breaking glass, which is what a Paramount security guard overheard as he was passing by. Later, the guard asked someone if they had heard the commotion and knew what was going on behind Arsenio's closed door. After word got out that the guard had overheard the fight, he was fired. Arsenio later quipped, "You know how people gossip."

Two years later, in September 1992, Shirley Ruiz would find herself in star-studded company when Arsenio stepped into the spotlight and blasted President Bush for his announcement that, although he was considering appearing on talk shows, he would bypass "The Arsenio Hall Show."

"Excuse me, George Herbert, irregular-heart-beating, read-my-lying-lipping, slipping-in-the-polls, do-nothing, deficit-raising, make-less-money-than-Millie-the-White-House-dog-last-year, Quayle-loving, sushi-puking Bush! I don't remember inviting your ass to my show . . . as a matter of fact, my ratings are higher than yours," an angry Arsenio told his astounded audience.

"At least I'm in good company," he added. "Now I've joined the ranks of the homeless, the unemployed, and the middle class. So I don't feel so bad."

The day after this verbal assault, Arsenio received approximately two hundred faxes and letters. Half of the missives were supportive, the other half denounced him.

No matter where one stood on the political front, Arsenio's monologue that night had to be considered an unnecessary and ugly slap at Bush. But most of all, it exposed the arrogance Arsenio had so successfully managed to hide from his adoring fans. It marked one of the few times that Arsenio's Mr. Nice Guy mask slipped, allowing the public a glimpse of the ego that lies beneath it. It is a vision usually reserved for his underlings and supposed enemies.

"In the beginning Arsenio was a nice guy," said a former show staff member. "But the more successful he became, the more spoiled and greedy he became. *Entertainment Weekly* said he was the most frenetic man in show business. And that's true. One day he's at your feet, kissing them, saying what a great job you are doing. The next day he'll be at your throat saying you haven't done enough for him lately.

"The more successful the show got, the more arrogant he got," the former staffer continued. "When he started out, he was happy to have any guest on the show that was available. Now he's so arrogant he truly believes Warren Beatty is 'lucky to have his ass on my couch,' as he once told several of us.

"Arsenio thinks he deserves big names. He doesn't understand they're guests. He thinks he's doing them a favor, not vice versa. But the main thing about Arsenio is that he's become very lazy where the show's concerned.

"He claims to watch the show three times after it's taped? Bullshit. He doesn't have time. He claims to do the research, the booking. He claims to do everything. But it's arrogance out of control. He is given the introduction and the background, the preinterview questions and answers, but he never reads the material. If he would just do his show, he would be fine, but he's got that movie deal with Paramount and he's just stretched too thin."

Arsenio has two preinterviewers and a research team who collect information on his guests, then present him with a synopsis of what they've learned. "I have everything from whom they slept with last night to what their grade-point average in high school was, if I choose to use it," he once bragged.

"That's true," confirmed a former staffer, "but when the segment producers go down to brief him about the guests, he frequently lays on his couch and pretends to be asleep, with his hat pulled down over his eyes and his eyes closed. He would never even come upstairs to talk to the staff, unless he was doing a prep interview . . . and even that was rare.

"It's this simple," the former member of Hall's inner sanctum explained. "When Arsenio first came on, there was a sort of charm to his naïveté. But it doesn't exist anymore. It's like his claim about being such a feminist and having so much respect and trust for women because he was raised by women. Maybe that was once the case, but it isn't any longer. He's surrounded by women because he feels it gives him more power.

"Let's just put it this way," the ex-staffer continued. "The staff loved him in the beginning. The first year, the first eighteen months, he was acceptable, a really good guy. Then came the bodyguards, the new offices, the bullet proof glass, and having to be buzzed into his office to see him.

"Now, if I had to sum up the staff's feeling about Arsenio, I'd say it was a combination of fear and dislike. And I think it's beginning to show on the air. How does that cliché go? 'You can fool half of the people some of the time, but you can't fool all of the people all of the time.' Well, I think the public and the press are slowly beginning to see behind the persona of Arsenio . . . and, frankly, it's not a very pretty picture."

CHAPTER

10

No matter how Arsenio has treated other people in his life, he has been a consistently loving son to his mother, a woman described as "a real sweetheart" by those who know her. When he first struck it rich in Hollywood, for example, he began sending a portion of his earnings to Annie Hall, who was still living in Chicago, but had left her union job and was working as a financial-aid counselor for the DeVries Institute of Technology, a vocational school.

A self-professed "mama's boy," he has always made a point of calling her daily since leaving home for college. "Sometimes," he once explained, "my biggest regret is that I can give her everything but time."

Thus, in 1983, when ABC reportedly paid him a $50,000 retainer and put him in that ill-fated ABC summer series "The Half Hour Comedy Hour," he paid off the loan on his mother's car, gave his Mustang to his girlfriend, Diane Roberts, and bought himself a shiny new Nissan Maxima.

In 1987 he purchased a new Nissan 240SX for his mother and a new white Jaguar for himself, explaining: "I love cars. The best thing to do when you want to think is to get in a car and drive. It's a good way to work your problems out. Eddie has a white Vette and I have a white Jag. We just get out, and let the top down, and go."

The following year, when his annual earnings jumped to $2.5 million, thanks to the Paramount contract, he gave his mother a West Hollywood condo on Kings Road as a Christmas present and moved her from the Windy City to sunny Los Angeles.

"My mother was a hard worker," he told associates. "That's why I've been so happy to be able to do the things for her now that I can. I've seen my mother cry many times because she couldn't buy me something for Christmas. She would cry, and I would console her."

Having gone through so much together, and being only twenty-three years apart in age, Arsenio and Annie Hall are exceptionally close, more like brother and sister than like mother and son. She is, according to Arsenio, an untraditional mother, unconcerned about his lingering bachelorhood. Of course, considering her one and only marriage and its sour conclusion, how could she be anything else?

Nevertheless, Arsenio is pleased that "she's not one of those mothers who's always trying to set me up, or asking me, 'When are you going to get married? When are you going to have children so I can have grandchildren?'"

She is his best friend, his confidante, and his most trusted critic. Together they form a tightly knit twosome whose loyalty to each other was forged in the ghetto fires of a Cleveland past.

"No one barks louder at my show than my mom," Arsenio has proudly bragged, adding: "She's my barometer of what works and what doesn't. My question always is, 'Does it make my mother laugh?'"

So when Annie Hall was moving west, he jokingly worried aloud that living in Los Angeles might make her too sophisticated for his own good. "She'll probably get hip and change her name to Bambi. Then I'll have to find another barometer," he'd laughed. And he was appalled when shortly after settling into the condo, she went out and had a photographer do a series of publicity head shots because she was interested in doing commercials.

By 1990, Annie Hall was living in a nice, but certainly unpretentious California ranch-style home in the San Fernando Valley, not far from the modest splendor of her only son's four-bedroom Hollywood Hills home. Decorated in his favorite color, blue, and filled with electronic gear, the house was his bastion of privacy, a large adult playroom and an obvious attempt to compensate for a childhood of meager luxuries.

"I'm very high-tech oriented. I wouldn't have a TV without doors that open electronically." The house not only had nine television sets, with and without doors, it also had a view of the valley, a swimming pool, and a room devoted entirely to his toys; Arsenio's teddy-bear collection, which had by then grown to three hundred thanks to the generosity of fans, filled various nooks in the rest of the house.

"The Christmas that I was nine," he explained, "my parents had divorced and we were short of money. My mother brought me a little stuffed dog for Christmas, and I was upset because I wanted other toys.

"So she sat me down and explained to me what Christmas is all about," he continued. "She told me about how it's the love and thought behind the gift that matters, not the money. I still have that dog, and now I can have any stuffed animal I want. It makes me remember where I came from."

Ah, but that was then. This is now. To listen to Arsenio, one would almost swear he'd never left the ghetto of Cleveland behind. The image of being a poor, black, struggling comic is one that he seems to revel in, whereas being a wealthy, successful comic seems to make him uncomfortable. Or at least it did. Or at least he liked to pretend it did. "I don't know what it is," he once confessed about his conservative spending habits and ever-increasing wealth. "I guess I'm just not used to it, and I'm a little afraid it's going to go away. I guess that's why I tend to live under my means. What goes up must come down, and it's a shorter fall if you live within your means."

To this end, Arsenio has frequently stated, "I'm not a splurger. If anything, I'm real cheap. I told my business manager, 'I want to get a Range Rover, but I hate to throw away money.' He said, 'Trust me, you can afford it.'"

Despite his protestations, however, in 1991, Arsenio added yet another car to his growing collection, which by then included a white 1986 Jaguar XJS and his black Mustang 5.0. The latest acquisition was an expensive dark blue Porsche Carrera, an ironic twist considering only the year before he had said: "The best thing about money is that it lets me have my privacy. People see me driving my Mustang and they say, 'You should get a Porsche, a Carrera.' I feel like saying, 'I'll buy you a Carrera just to get you away from me.'"

Ah, but what good is life if you make millions of dollars a year and don't spend it? And by 1991 Arsenio was very, very rich. In fact he had been named the third wealthiest talk-show host on television, earning $12 million annually right behind Oprah Winfrey with her staggering $38 million yearly income.

So only a year after having described himself as a man devoted to modest living, Arsenio was reported to have purchased the long time Hollywood Hills home of the late crooner Rudy Vallee.

The pink Spanish-style hacienda built in the thirties, consisted of five bedrooms, six baths, a theater, game room, several secret passages and roof terrace, as well as a pool, a tennis court, and a 360-degree view of the San Fernando Valley. Nevertheless, Arsenio didn't feel the house was adequate for his needs. It was not, in his estimation, stylish enough for a reigning prince of late night such as himself.

In early December 1991, within days of the escrow closing, he began demolishing the six-thounsand-square-foot house. In its place was to be a fifteen-thousand-square-foot mansion, designed specifically by Arsenio for Arsenio. As one neighbor commented, "This guy doesn't even have a family. That place is massive for just one man."

What had been a secluded area, where deer and coyotes occasionally roam, was shattered with the sounds of construction crews. The lot was graded and trees cut down to make way for a putting green and tennis court. And because there was a need for more fill dirt, ten trucks made daily trips up and down the hill for the next three months, hauling in a reported nine thousand tons of soil.

Despite the noise and unusually heavy traffic, the neighbors did not complain until they discovered Arsenio was planning to replace the old tennis court. The planned new court was designed to sit atop five concrete pilings above an underground driveway, the tennis court would have blocked the sun from the yards of the houses below. With the shadow of the proposed court hovering over their homes, the residents would have found themselves living in a valley rather than on a hill, and their property values would have plummeted. At that point, they decided to take action, and Arsenio once again found himself in the middle of a controversy.

"I think he thought that he was going to be able to put over a fast one and get everything done before we realized what was happening," confided one of the neighbors. But it wasn't to be.

More than one hundred residents of the Mulholland Drive neighborhood, including actors Martin Landau and Robert Carradine, complained to the zoning board about Arsenio's home improvement and landscaping plans.

Perched on huge twenty-five-foot-high concrete pilings, the proposed tennis court, they explained, would loom over their properties, blocking the daylight and creating a hazard during California's rainy season. It would be, explained Blue Andre, a movie producer, like having a battleship above my property.

"I don't want to stop his house," Andre added, "I just want to stop this monster tennis court."

Charlotte Antelinne, a spokeswoman for the Cahuenga Pass Property Owners Association said, the "Great Tennis Court Controversy" had become a disturbing symbol of how overdevelopment was destroying a way of life. "This mansionization of the hills and canyons around Los Angeles has got to stop," she said. "Building houses the size of hotels blocks other people's viewers, light, and privacy—all the things people move to the area for."

The rest of the neighborhood echoed her sentiments. Throughout the controversy Arsenio kept a low profile, at one point even denying he had purchased the estate. "I just spoke to Arsenio, and he knows nothing about the situation," Dana Freedman later told the press.

After several hearings, the zoning board agreed with the neighbors. And Arsenio, even though he had originally gained a zoning variance for the tennis court, was informed he would have to find another location for the court on his two-and-a-half-acre estate.

One can only imagine, then, just how surprised the rebellious neighbors were when, not long after the *Los Angeles Times* had run a lengthy story on the feud, Arsenio announced that he *had* purchased the Vallee estate . . . but merely as an investment and that he had no plans of living there.

"I'm a frugal and cautious purchaser," he had explained, adding with a laugh, "I'm actually borderline cheap. But I have no problem buying property. I have a partnership business, and we buy a lot of real estate to turn around.

"I also have different methods of saving—bonds and so forth—depending on what's doing well. And I'm slowly making an attempt to become educated in the field of stocks. But most of my money goes into real estate."

Moreover, despite a *Los Angeles Times* story to the contrary, Arsenio denied ever having surveyed the Vallee estate from a helicopter. "I'm afraid to fly and I've never been in a helicopter, with God as my witness," he said. "There's not even a gray area there.

"I have this mortality thing," he continued, "an incredible fear of death. You know, when you're playing basketball, you get bumped around a lot, you get elbowed, and the next day you'll say 'Ouch!' while you're reaching for something? Well, I go crazy. 'Cancer! Heart attack! I'm going to die!' I'm in the doctor's office and I go, 'What is that?' And he says, 'It's a bruise.'"

Neighbors believed Arsenio *had* purchased the Vallee estate to live in. And, according to reporters, he had flown over the property in a helicopter, like his good friend Jerry Buss, owner of the Los Angeles Lakers basketball team, had done when he purchased Pickfair, the legendary Beverly Hills estate of Douglas Fairbanks and Mary Pickford.

Arsenio also had met with Eleanor Vallee, Rudy's widow, who had lived in the home, which had been built in 1930 for film star Ann Harding, for forty years after her marriage to the legendary crooner and who had sold it believing that it would be preserved.

When Rudy died at eighty-five in 1986, the estate had gone on the market for $10 million. Nine months later it had been reduced to $5.5 million. It remained on the market until Arsenio came along in 1991 and picked it up through a trust for $3.5 million in cash.

By the time the estate was finally sold, Eleanor Vallee had married attorney Edward Hustedt and was living in a condo in Brentwood. "I don't really want to sell it," she had said of the house, "but I'm ready to go on with a new life."

According to friends, when Eleanor discovered what Arsenio was doing to her beautiful home, she was furious. She could not believe that the charming, well-mannered, seemingly sincere man she had met could have led her to believe that he had no plans of changing anything, other than adding a fourth-story master-bedroom suite so that he could have an even better view of the San Fernando valley and the Los Angeles basin.

But the fact that construction on the house had begun within days of the escrow closing meant that Arsenio had the plans drawn up and the permits in place all the while he had been negotiating with her.

"I think he thought he could pull a fast one and that by the time the neighbors realized what was going on it would be too late for them to stop him," confided a neighbor and a longtime friend of Eleanor Vallee. "He had the permits, the plans, everything was in place. I don't think he believed the zoning board could—or would—stop him."

But, of course, they did stop him. And now the estate is in a shambles. Angry about having his plans thwarted, Arsenio stopped all work. It was then, and only then, that Arsenio had finally admitted he had, indeed, purchased the property . . . but only as an investment.

If there's speculation, innuendo, and confusion about Arsenio's personal life, and there has been a great deal during the past couple of years, it's because he has carefully veiled it fromt he public. As a result, only a very few friends even know where Arsenio lives, or how he lives, let alone who, if anyone, he is living with.

He is, in fact, so secretive about his private life that he is one of the few celebrities ever to have turned down a Barbara Walters interview because she wanted to conduct it at his home.

"Yeah," he once admitted, "I must be one of two retards who turned down the Barbara Walters show. I give you all of me as an entertainer. I give you none of me as a private person. I have to have something that's all mine, and that's my love life, my home life.

My bed and my house—that's all I keep. Eddie did something with Barbara in his bedroom. It's not wrong. I'm just different.

"I've said everything from [the fact that]my ultimate fantasy is to sleep with two women to my dad slapped my mother. So the bottom line is sometimes I give a little bit, sometimes I give none."

"Who I'm sleeping with—who I'm really sleeping with—you will never know," he continued. "In fact, despite stories to the contrary, I've never been in love with a performer or had a serious relationship with a performer.

"I'm finished with show-business women," he laughed. "No more pop singers for me. I've tried that a couple of times, but two-show business egos in the house doesn't work. It's hard enough just to deal with one package of show-business pains. I have had awful, awful luck with show-business women."

Nevertheless, in the last eight years he has been romantically linked, at least in the press, with several Hollywood beauties, including Emma Samms, the "Dynasty" vixen; Mary Frann, of "Newhart" fame; Leslie Bega, a star of ABC's "Head of the Class" series; songstress Whitney Houston; dancer Paula Abdul; and singer-songwriter Sinead O'Connor, to name only a few.

"We dated in 1984," Arsenio recently admitted when asked about his relationship with Emma, "but I knew going out with a white person wasn't cool career-wise, so I told her we had to eat at McDonald's and keep it low-key."

And what about Leslie Bega, who was eleven years his junior when the twosome was seen partying around Los Angeles in the summer of 1988?

Through a spokesperson, Arsenio had denied a romantic liaison with the young blond actress. "We're just friends," he said. However, a member of Leslie's family admitted the two were "very, very close. I just hope he doesn't break her heart," the concerned relative added.

And Mary Frann? "I only took her to one party."

And Paula Abdul, whom Arsenio once greeted at the Los Angeles airport with a single red rose? The two had become an item after meeting during the filming of *Coming to America* when Abdul was hired to choreograph a dance sequence.

"Paula and I are very good friends, very tight. We have been to dinner. We have been seen in places together. But as close as we were, Paula needed a man who would put her first."

And Whitney Houston? "The stories about Whitney got started because I did jokes about being her 'love machine' in my monologue on the show. One night I came out and said, 'I'm sorry. It's a joke.' And she came out behind me and said, 'No, it's not a joke. I'm pregnant.' The crowd went nuts, and the rumors started."

Arsenio had managed to create a similar situation in October 1989 when, spotted by the paparazzi having lunch with Paula Abdul, he jokingly announced that the two had secretly just gotten married.

"That story spread like wildfire and now," Abdul complained at the time, "everyone in America is convinced we're married. Arsenio is a practical joker, and that was his idea of a real laugh," she confided. "But it made me really mad because now men think I'm spoken for, and they're scared to approach me."

The dating game apparently proved to be less difficult than Paula had imagined. She became engaged to actor John Stamos less than nine months later. And although that marriage did not take place, she supposedly had asked Arsenio to be best man—which was what Madonna had been teasing Arsenio about during her first appearance on his show.

In May 1990, tabloid rumors of a romance with Janet Jackson turned out to nothing, even though the twosome was seen emerging from a Los Angeles hotel elevator holding hands.

Six months later similar rumors surfaced about Arsenio and actress Maria Conchita Alonso, a former Miss Venezuela, when the twosome attended the Los Angeles premiere of *Honeymoon in Vegas* together. But as in the case of Janet Jackson, Maria denied the rumors of a blossoming romance, claiming the two were "just good pals."

And in the spring of 1991, Arsenio was rumored to be in the midst of "a red-hot romance" with none other than Sinead O'Connor, the controversial Irish singer-songwriter of sans hair fame, after the dynamic duo were seen dining at the Ivy, a trendy West Hollywood eatery.

Segueing from dinner to the Comedy Store, the odd couple were reportedly seen hugging and cuddling and kissing in a darkened corner. The supposed romance was either short-lived or amounted to nothing because, in this case, no one from either side even bothered to contradict the gossip.

Nor did Arsenio confirm or deny 1992 reports that he was living with Rosalia Hayakawa, a beautiful bit-part actress, whom he supposedly had moved into his Hollywood Hills home and had introduced to guests at an Eddie Murphy party as "my future wife."

According to a Hall associate, Arsenio met Rosalia

in 1989 at a nightclub and had dated her off and on until 1991, when he decided he was in love with her. "This is for real. For keeps," the friend said. "I've never seen Arsenio so committed to one woman."

As for Arsenio, he isn't talking about Rosalia or any of his other supposed girlfriends . . . not now and probably not ever. He has consistently denied reports about his romantic liaisons as far back as his earliest days in Los Angeles. Take, for example, his heartrending story of a six-year relation-ship with a high- school sweetheart, unnamed, of course— which supposedly ended because of his desire for a show-business career in Los Angeles.

"We had lived together through college, and when we graduated, we'd moved away and got a job together. This was a six-year relationship that ended because I got into this business. She said, 'That's not me. You're from Cleveland with dreams of being a star. I'm just from Cleveland.'"

It's a poignant story, but unfortunately, like so many of Arsenio's tales, it's entirely not true. According to several Chicagoans who were close to Arsenio during the two years he spent in the Windy City, although he never lacked for girlfriends, most of whom were white, they never knew of any college sweetheart to whom he was devoted.

Arsenio has always insisted that women are a low priority on his list of personal wants.

"I am the most undersexed guy on the planet," he confided in a 1987 interview, proving again what a terrific sense of humor he really does have. "If a girl is with me, she gets it twice a month max."

Yet in another interview that same year, he explained that " Although I'm a healthy, single guy, I have my duties, part of which is I can't be promiscuous or not wear a condom. If I ever fouled up," he added, "I know there'd be some kid out there saying, 'I thought he was the one guy we could trust.'"

In 1988, however, he confessed he had been celibate for almost a year due to his heavy work schedule. "Relationships," he had explained, "are very hard to make work when you're doing what I'm doing. Show business," he had added, "is like a woman who will leave you if you don't give her attention and love and caring. I don't want to have to say, 'Babe, you're the chick on the side.'"

Still another explanation for his single status has been that he's a loner who can't imagine being married. "I don't think I could ever live with someone," he has said innumerable times. "I can be around a woman for forty-eight hours; around the forty-nineth hour, I leave her. I can't get married. I'm a loner and I like my time to myself.

"My life is in front of people, so when I go home, I don't want to hear voices," he confided. "There's nobody in my house that'll tell me I can't make it, because there ain't nobody there. I'm alone. And I'm happy being alone. That's how you insulate yourself from negativity."

In late 1988, however, Arsenio confided to an *Ebony* magazine writer that he was involved in an exclusive relationship with a twenty-one-year-old former credit analyst and part-time college student who, prior to moving in with him, had worked with his mother. He refused to divulge her name, though. "I made the choice to be in the spotlight, she didn't," he explained, parroting a Bill Cosby line of yesteryear.

More recently he's confessed that he would "love to be married and to have a kid. But I don't feel I'd be a good father right now because I'm very selfish with this career thing I'm obsessed with. I'm not even a good boyfriend."

In June 1992, Arsenio confessed to enjoying chasing butterflies with his goddaughter, Bria, Eddie Murphy's daughter, and to wanting a child of his own. "When I get my lowest," he said, "it's because I realize all my buddies—Eddie and Magic—have kids. I want a kid so bad. I am the product of a single-parent household, but I'd like to do this in the traditional way. I'm trying to have a family-values fairy tale. But in this business you have to be real careful. You can't just bring a kid into your life.

"So," he concluded, "when I can't take it anymore and I need a daughter, that's when I'm going to have to settle down and get married."

However, only the year before he had confided: "I have never had a person tell me the upside of marriage. All I know are downsides. I'm not as clear on kids as I am on marriage. Sometimes I think about having a kid, but I'm not planning on it at this point, and I can do that without marriage."

What does all of this add up to, other than confusion?

It adds up to fear, the kind of fear that has Arsenio, in an effort to keep his fans from knowing his moves, frequently spending the night at his Kings Road condominium in West Hollywood, which he had originally purchased for his mother. "He's constantly changing his routine in case anyone is stalking him," confided an associate. "He doesn't want to go the way Rebecca Schaeffer went, shot and killed by some crazy fan who found out where she lived."

It adds up to the fact that Arsenio is a very well-known black entertainer who doesn't want his adoring public to know much about his off-camera life and that the majority of his girlfriends have been white.

Most of all, it adds up to Arsenio having created and nurtured a public persona which is far different than how he really behaves when not in front of the public.

A perfect example of this can be found in his oft-stated comments about how much he respects and likes women, since he was raised by three of them. As one former employee of "The Arsenio Hall Show" so pointedly summed it up: "I mean, really. How much respect do you have when you give women black dildos with a watch wrapped around them as Christmas presents? One of the women didn't think it was funny and returned it immediately. The others didn't think it was funny, but they didn't have the guts to give it back to him."

CHAPTER

11

The bells heralding the beginning of 1991 had barely quit ringing when Arsenio launched the first TV project under his new Wachs-negotiated agreement with Paramount. Titled "The Party Machine with Nia Peeples," the show was a nightly half hour of music and dance designed to capture a late-night audience tired of talk, but not too exhausted to party hearty.

"I used to wake up Saturday morning after a night out on the town and watch those TV dance shows, and I always thought there was something wrong there," Arsenio explained. "No one is usually dancing or partying on Saturday morning. They're eating breakfast."

An alumna on the TV series, "Fame" and host of the short-lived CBS late-night show, "Tops of the Pops," as well as a recording artist and host of MTV's "Street Scene," Peeples had met Arsenio at a party the year before "Party" began. She had never even been a guest on his show when he tapped her for the head partier on the new show.

"Nia's beautiful, intelligent, the smartest, most versatile, gorgeous woman in her category, and I know them all. She dances, she sings, she acts, she's a mother, and you're looking at the face of an angel. This girl should be huge," Arsenio had waxed enthusiastically just prior to the show's debut.

Despite Arsenio's exuberant belief in Peeples, she had been reluctant, at first anyway, to host the show. "I was kind of leery," the twenty-nine-year-old actress said shortly before the show's premiere. "I didn't want to be Arsenio Hall. I'm not a stand-up comedian."

But Arsenio prevailed, and Peeples signed on.

"The whole idea," she explained to the press, "is that it's an 'after' party for Arsenio's show. He wants the feel of people hanging out and having a good time, with something good to look at—which for him is beautiful bodies dancing."

Thus, armed with a multimillion-dollar contract from Paramount, Arsenio put his clout behind a late-night party of his own. "The Party Machine" was sold, along with Arsenio's show, as a ninety-minute package, which offered the nation's independent TV stations an inexpensive opportunity to compete with NBC's blockbuster late-night lineup of "the Tonight Show" and "Late Night with David Letterman."

"Whenever I go out, whether it's to the Grammy Awards or the NAACP Image Awards," Arsenio explained, "people always ask, 'Where's the party?' That's what 'The Party Machine' will be—a show for people who want the party to continue and don't want to hear any more talking."

Despite the talents of Nia Peeples, however, and occasional appearances by Arsenio in a last- minute ploy to salvage the ratings, "The Party Machine" was a short-lived disaster. Eight months after it began, the party ended, not with a bang, but with a gong. No one, it seemed, wanted to party late into the night on weekdays. Arsenio had originally blamed the venture's poor showing, as well as the temporary decline in his own Nielsen numbers, on the Persian Gulf War, which had also made its debut in January. But even after the war ended, the party barely alingered on.

In late June, Arsenio announced that the show would end in September. "I wasn't giving my station managers what I'd promised," he explained, "and my relations with those stations is very important. I'd rather cut off my finger and save my arm. So the decision has been made. We're going to pull the plug while we're still in love."

By that time Arsenio had also pulled the plug on a Cleveland Pizza parlor bearing his name and even having the chutzpah to serve a "Let's Get Busy" burger.

Arsenio first learned about "Arsenio's Pizza and Ribs," the name of the restaurant, when his mother saw the place while visiting some friends in the old Cleveland neighborhood. "Then I started getting letters from people about it," Arsenio later explained, "and I started wondering, 'What's next? Somebody chokes on a piece of pizza crust and I get sued?'"

"I mean, they put it in my old neighborhood! I had friends calling and teasing me: 'Yo, man, I had the collard-green pizza the other day, with the hamhock calzone.' Pizza and ribs, man, that sounds like a joke."

Not wanting the joke to be on him, Arsenio instructed his attorney, Howard King, to file suit against the Cleveland restaurant's owners for having borrowed his name without his permission. "Arsenio is hardly a common, garden-variety name," King told the inquisitive press. "The guy was obviously trying to trade on Arsenio's name and create the mistaken impression that it was somehow Arsenio's restaurant by opening it in his hometown, in his old neighborhood."

Filed February 5, 1991, in U.S. District Court in Cleveland, the suit named Arsenio's Pizza Inc., which had been operating the restaurant since June 1990, at 7511 Kinsman Road, only four blocks away from where Arsenio grew up, and the restaurant's co-owners, Mazan Rabah and Steven Fenker, neither of whom was happy about finding themselves in court and in the headlines.

"He made it big and here we are trying to eke out a little business, I think it's wrong what he's doing," Mazan Rabah complained. "We have nothing to do with him. It's our right to use any name we want. We're prepared to defend ourselves in court. The lawsuit is ludicrous. How he feels he's helping us sell pizza is beyond me."

Fortunately for Arsenio, the Cleveland judge did not agree with Rabah's assessment. He ordered the owners to change the name of the restaurant. Considering Arsenio's previous court battles, first with Willis Edwards of the Hollywood NAACP, and then with his then-manager, Robert Wachs, this case was a piece of legal cake.

Like the two years that preceded it, 1991 was not without threats against his life or strange incidents on the set. In February, for instance, two young men in the audience hurled a chemical compound on stage, staining the furniture and clothing of several crew members and injuring a dozen members of the audience.

According to a crew member, there was a crackling sound just as Arsenio was concluding his monologue. Hall looked up and told the audience, "It must be the lights." He then told his last joke and the show broke for a commercial. Before it resumed, the two men had been arrested. It was, they told police, "only a prank."

But despite the pizza suit, the failure of "The Party Machine," and the so-called prank, the big news of 1991, as far as Arsenio was concerned, occurred on the afternoon of November 7, 1991, when Earvin "Magic" Johnson, one of his two best friends, appeared for a hastily called press conference at the Great Western Forum in Inglewood to announce that he was retiring from basketball because he had tested positive for the HIV virus.

"I just want to make it clear first of all that I do not have the AIDS disease," Johnson told the stunned group. "I plan on being here for a long time. Life is going to go on for me and I'm going to be a happy man. But sometimes you're a little naive and think something like this is not going to happen to you. You think it only happens to other people. But here I am, saying that it can happen to anybody. Even me, Magic Johnson."

Although Magic appeared calm and self-confident and even occasionally managed to flash his ingenuous smile during the televised press conference, Arsenio knew just how deeply his friend had been shaken by the news. Arsenio had been one of the first people Magic had telephoned after the discovery during a routine physical examination.

Stunned by the news, Arsenio had repeatedly asked him if he was absolutely positive the test results were correct. Magic had assured him that having taken the AIDS test twice, he was convinced he was carrying the virus. Arsenio was speechless.

Although he had managed to maintain an outward calm for Magic's sake, the truth was that Arsenio was absolutely terrified as he hung up the phone. He was frightened for what lay ahead for Magic and afraid that having had numerous sexual encounters himself, he might also be infected.

Despite his words to the contrary—"It hasn't changed me, nor has it scared me," he told the press, explaining he had been dating the same woman for a year and didn't feel he needed to be tested—Arsenio did place a call to his minister, the Reverend Cecil Murray, at the AME Church in South Central Los Angeles, where he spent hours in the ensuing days praying . . . for Magic and, most probably, for himself.

Several days later Arsenio watched as Magic bravely shared his illness with the rest of the disbelieving world. He was barely able to tear himself away from the TV monitor in his Paramount office to prepare for that night's taping. But he did, because by the time Magic had held his press conference, Arsenio had already invited him to appear on the show, and Magic had accepted.

With Roseanne Arnold booked to discuss her childhood incest and Magic discussing AIDS, it was going to be a heavy-duty show. Arsenio hoped he could make it through the taping without losing his cool. It had been difficult enough just talking to the press about Magic's illness. "It's obviously a wake-up call to the world," he'd repeatedly told reporters. "I'm just devastated that the alarm clock was my partner."

And Arsenio was truly devastated by Magic's announcement. Eddie Murphy might be like a brother to him, but in the years since they'd first met, Magic had become his best friend.

Thus there was no opening monologue on the night of November 8, 1991. Instead the curtains opened to Arsenio and Magic sitting together, Arsenio in his chair, Magic on the couch. It had only been twenty-four hours since Magic's press conference. The audience went wild, clapping, cheering, and chanting in a five-minute standing ovation that seemed as though it would never end.

"I didn't want to do a monologue that night," Arsenio later explained. "What's funny after you find out somebody you care about, respect, and love has been diagnosed HIV positive?"

While nine million American households watched, Magic discussed the AIDS virus, what it had done to his life, told the audience he had contracted the disease through heterosexual contact, that his wife, Cookie, did not have the virus, that he would go on with his life, and that he would welcome an opportunity to serve on President Bush's National Commission on AIDS.

It was one of Arsenio's highest-rated shows and, certainly, a testament to Magic's stature as one of the world's finest and best-liked athletes. But to Arsenio, it was one of the most difficult situations he had ever experienced.

"It was the hardest show I've ever done, and I don't believe there'll be a harder show in my life," he would later tell interviewers. "That day was like the day I heard Martin Luther King was dead. There was a somber attitude in department stores. It was on every news station, on everybody's lips. Magic has a strength and courage that flow from his positive attitude and his smile, and I knew my job was to deliver that to America.

"Since I knew there were going to be some very

unethical and unkind things said at some point, I wanted to let him tell his story. We had a lot of guests booked that night. Roseanne and Tom Arnold called me and said, 'We'll come, we'll be there, but if he wants our time, he can have it.'

"Keep in mind, Magic's thing dwarfed everything, but Roseanne had a serious thing to talk about, too. By the time he came on, I had cried myself out."

Arsenio and Magic had met through a mutual friend in the early eighties, not long after Arsenio moved to the West Coast. Over the years they had become close friends. It was, in fact, a natural bonding of two men who shared a love of basketball, a love of laughter, and definitely a love of women.

"When I first came out here," Arsenio once recalled, "we had a mutual friend who said, 'You want to go to a basketball game? Magic Johnson's a friend of mine.' At the end of the game, we went downstairs, and he was coming out of the locker room, and he said, 'Yo! The guy from the Comedy Store!' Then he asked, 'Where did you sit?' And I said, 'You see this blood dripping out of my nose? I was REAL high up. Some stewardess from American Airlines came by with peanuts and shit!'

"We joked and fooled around and he was laughing. The next day, our mutual friend said 'Magic says if you ever want tickets, call him.' So he'd come to the Comedy Store, and I'd get him a good seat; and I'd go to the games, and he'd get me a good seat. And that's really how it happened.

"We became friends. He's a really special, unselfish kind of guy. I don't use the word 'friend' loosely, because I think people use it too much. If I have enough friends to count on one hand, I'm a very lucky man. And Magic's one of those friends."

In the days that followed Magic's disclosure of his diagnosis, Arsenio repeatedly asked him what he could do to help. "I'll do anything you ask," he'd say. "Just tell me what it is."

Finally Magic suggested the two of them produce and star in a video about AIDS awareness. Arsenio agreed, later explaining,

"I wanted to do something, anything, that would help wipe out ignorance about AIDS," he explained, adding, "This is not a project for children. This is an adult approach to safe sex, abstinence, monogamy, and knowledge. There are people who don't know how to put on a condom."

Titled *Time Out: The Truth About HIV, AIDS and You*, the video was released in October, 1992 only eleven months after Magic's startling announcement. A hip primer on how to avoid the AIDS virus, the video was forty-two minutes of rock, rap, and biting comedy interspersed with straight talk about everything from HIV testing to the finer points of using a condom.

Arsenio pulled out all the stops on the video, gathering an impressive array of celebrities to get Magic's message across. The video featured guest appearances by Paula Abdul, Kirstie Alley, Mayim Bialik, Johnny Gill, Sinbad, Jasmine Guy, and Kadeem Hardison, as well as Luke Perry, Pauly Shore, Jaleel White, and Malcolm-Jamal Warner, Bill Cosby's favorite TV son, who also directed the video.

The lineup of guests was a testament to Arsenio's clout in the entertainment world, as well as to his increased desire to wield that power for the betterment of mankind, specifically the black community.

By the time the video was released, Arsenio had become a founding board member of the Magic Johnson Foundation, a nonprofit organization to fund pediatric AIDS research, and he also was on the board of Starlight Foundation, an organization founded by actress Emma Samms, his former girl-friend, to grant dying children their last wish.

"I met a Starlight kid who was just thrilled to see me," he recalled not long ago, "but the mother was not very happy. The little girl said, 'My parents call me Latifah 'cause I like you so much. They tease me and say I wanted to be born black.' That's some deep shit to put on a kid. Cruel shit. There's a parent ragging a sick kid 'cause she likes me and I'm black and she's white? That was the strangest curve any-body ever threw me."

Arsenio is an active participant in both Starlight and the Make A Wish Foundation because, he explains, "It keeps my ego in control, and keeps me out of trouble."

But the organization closest to his heart is DARE, a nonprofit Drug Abuse Resistance Education program attempting to educate grade-school children about the dangers of drug use. As the organization's national ambassador since 1990, Arsenio has spent a great deal of his time during the past three years traveling the country to visit DARE classrooms and taping radio and television public-service commercials.

"I have worked for the past couple of years with organizations that help keep young people away from drugs and alcohol," Arsenio stated in a recent Paramount press release explaining his affiliation with DARE. "In 1989," the release continued, "I chose to do a series of public-service announcements

for the TARGET organization, where I interviewed
youths who had experienced, firsthand, the devastating effects of drug abuse. It really made me take a
hard look at the drug situation, which has obviously
reached overwhelming proportions.

"I don't think that we will ever be able to elimi-
nate the pushers or the influx of illegal drugs being
smuggled into our country," the release concluded.
"We can, however, through programs like DARE,
educate our young people and help them to build
the kind of self-esteem that will enable them to stay
away from drugs."

Anyone reading that masterfully conceived press
release, or listening to Arsenio's various antidrug
messages, could only conclude that the talk-show
host lives a drug-free life, especially since he'd even
admitted in print that he'd tried marijuana once,
maybe even twice, as a college student and hadn't
found it to be a rewarding experience.

"Yeah, I smoked a joint one time, in college," he
had conceded in a 1992 interview. "And, yeah, I
inhaled. But it didn't do anything for me."

Thus it would be unimaginable that this pillar of
straightforward talk, this Sunday-go-to-meeting
supporter of the All-American Dream, this stalwart
role model for the black community would himself
use drugs. And yet, according to someone who has
known him since he first arrived in Los Angeles,
Arsenio was "a heavy user" of cocaine throughout
the eighties and, according to a former Hall show
staffer, he was still snorting coke as recently as
January 1992.

"Yeah, I'd say he had a habit in the eighties," a
former participant in Arsenio's late-night/early-morn-
ing cokefests confided. "He liked to drink, too. And

when he'd drink and do drugs, he could get real nasty, real fast. He has a bad temper and could go off in a minute. He'd get real insulting and rude to people, too. He just wasn't nice to be around at those times, you know?"

According to another former intimate, Arsenio sometimes had coke before taping his show, but more often afterward. "He always had at least one, sometimes two, shots of Jack Daniel's prior to doing the show. And, yes, I've seen him occasionally do coke along with the alcohol, which is why I think it's the combination of the coke and the alcohol that creates his terrible mood swings. He's up, he's down. You never know which it's going to be."

No wonder Arsenio has been so vociferous in describing the restrictions placed upon his padded shoulders as a role model for the black community. "It's not easy being Arsenio Hall," he has admitted. "There are so many temptations out here in Hollywood, and I've got to live my life right and be a role model. I've got to wear a condom, not be promiscuous, and keep cocaine out of my life.

"There are parties I don't go to, people I don't hang out with, because I have to set an example," he continued. "I can't be in their house because I know what goes on in there. There are people counting on me. If I get busted, if I end up in jail next to Todd Bridges, it would devastating," he concluded, "especially for a kid to look and say, 'He was the one I thought I could trust.'"

And therein lies a further explanation of why Arsenio works so hard to keep his personal life separate from his high-profile professional activities. No one ever said being in the spotlight was easy.

"Beneath it all I am just a guy who wants to make

people laugh," he says. "I am a comic, nothing more. However, I know that I have to do some things other than party, drive Porsches, snort coke, and get in Jacuzzis with beautiful women I've never met."

While it's true that Arsenio has devoted time, energy, and money to a variety of worthwhile causes, it's also true that beneath the smiling exterior, the mischievous little boy, and the humor, there rests the soul of a man who can prevaricate and never look back.

What's amazing is that Arsenio has so successfully managed to hide behind his carefully manufactured public persona for so long. Part of the reason, of course, is that although the entertainment industry has come to realize what Arsenio really is as a human being, no one is prepared to cast the first stone, especially if they happen to be white. After all, Arsenio has taken finger pointing to a new height, blaming white America anytime something doesn't go his way.

Moreover, what black member of the entertainment industry is going to step out on a limb and tarnish what has become the golden goose? After all, Arsenio has managed to rise to television heights few other African Americans have visited and, in doing so, has created a solid platform of exposure where there once was none.

Also, many people have remained quietly infuriated by Arsenio's growing arrogance and kinky hypocrisy from fear of retribution, especially if they work in the entertainment industry. As one former friend confided, "Anyone with the money, the power, and the temper that Arsenio has can be dangerous."

So Arsenio has blithely grown increasingly cocky with each passing season, talking more and more about sex and drugs on the air, and becoming increasingly incautious about protecting his carefully nurtured image. Whereas he had once listened to his advisers, to Lucie Salhany when she was at Paramount, and to producer Marla Kell Brown, Arsenio Hall no longer listens to anyone but himself.

By the end of 1991, Arsenio had become a man unleashed. There was no one, not even Eddie Murphy, who was funnier, more clever, more intelligent, or more powerful than Arsenio Hall. He had, to paraphrase a Hollywood joke, become a legend in his own mind.

CHAPTER

12

"'The Tonight Show' is an institution," Steve Allen said several years ago. "But with each tick of the clock, its advantage disappears. 'The Tonight Show' audience is dying every day."

Allen knew of what he was speaking. After all, in 1954, he had essentially created the talk-show format, as well as launched the venerable "Tonight Show."

Mel Harris, president of Paramount TV, agreed with Allen's assessment, which is why the studio was so enthusiastic about developing a late-night talk show with Arsenio in 1989. "In the 1960s, Johnny Carson started with a young audience that stuck with him for twenty years," Harris had pointed out. "Arsenio's is the new generation."

By the time Arsenio made his debut on January 3, 1989 "the Tonight Show" had been on the air for twenty-six successful years and had a perfect record of sinking the competition. This was true during Allen's, Jack Paar's, and Johnny Carson's reigns as King of Late Night.

Merv Griffin, Jerry Lewis, Joan Rivers, David Brenner, Joey Bishop, Les Crane, Ron Reagan, Jr., Rick Dees, Alan Thicke, and more recently Dennis Miller had all proven to be costly failures in what the television industry had long ago begun calling the "suicide slot."

Arsenio had outlasted them all. He had even defeated Pat Sajak, who, with the mighty CBS network behind him, had debuted as the host of his own late-night network show on January 9, 1989, only a week after Arsenio. Arsenio despised Sajak, but he never felt half the anger toward him that he felt toward Jay Leno when NBC announced he would be taking over "the Tonight Show" upon Johnny Carson's retirement in late May 1992. It was, quite simply, more than Arsenio could stand and he immediately went on the offensive, throwing verbal punches at Leno at every opportunity *before* Carson stepped down from the late-show podium.

Although his highly publicized feuds had garnered reams of press coverage, especially in the tabloids that feed on such disputes, it wasn't until Arsenio began attacking Leno that he really hit the big time in media coverage.

Beginning in early 1991, hardly a week passed when a magazine, newspaper, radio, or TV station didn't carry at least one story concerning Arsenio's thoughts about Leno or the behind-the-scenes machinations of the late-night talk-show battle for top celebrity guests and high ratings.

For reasons possibly beyond even his own grasp, Arsenio had leaped into the late-show arena, positioning himself as a righteous gladiator in a contest no one even suspected had existed until he burst forth, mouth roaring, to denounce Leno as someone beneath, way inheriting "the Tonight Show" throne.

Arsenio was angry that NBC tapped Leno as Carson's successor. After all, Johnny Carson was "the architect" of *his* dreams, not Jay Leno's. "The Tonight Show" should have been *his* legacy, not Jay's. Hadn't he devoted his entire life to emulating Carson? Hadn't he worked his black ass off to show white America that an African-American man could put his imprint on late-night talk television?

Did Jay Leno play the drums? Did he have a flair for magic? Had he spent his childhood in a ghetto apartment, watching Johnny, dreaming about being like Johnny, about having his own talk show? No. No. And no. It wasn't fair, it wasn't right. "The Tonight Show" should have been his, not Jay's.

Arsenio must have known he would never succeed Carson. But in his heart he had somehow always believed that it was his calling, his divine right, to sit in Johnny's chair behind Johnny's desk. When it didn't happen, and Arsenio knew it wasn't going to happen, he was furious. He liked Jay okay, but he saw him as being too nice, too weak, to replace his idol. Besides, in Arsenio's eyes, Jay hadn't really worked to get where he'd gotten. Not like Arsenio had worked. No, Jay didn't deserve "the Tonight Show".

So, operating on an emotional level that he could not even begin to explain to himself let alone anyone else, Arsenio lashed out at Leno and began an ongoing battle for late-night supremacy, which, dubbed the "Star Wars" by a fascinated media, continues to dominate coverage of the television industry today.

"What Carson has had is over—the dynasty is over, the control of one host over a nation is over," he told an interviewer. "I think we're all going to be jockeying for numbers and positions because Johnny Carson had a certain impact and control on our nation that I don't think anyone else will have.

"I think when Johnny leaves I'm going to be able to keep my core audience, and I'm going to be fine. I don't think any one man will ever occupy the demographics he has for twenty-nine years. I think everyone who made up that Carson number will just go everywhere. Some will take up crocheting, some will watch Dennis Miller, some will watch Jay Leno, some will rent more videocassettes. But no one will ever dominate like Johnny."

The first hint of the battle came in mid-1991 when, shortly after Carson officially announced his retirement, Arsenio declared, "Once Johnny steps down, it's going to be hardball" during an NBC interview with Maria Shriver.

But Arsenio didn't wait for Carson's departure to begin playing the game. Only a week or two after Carson's announcement, Arsenio's producers attempted to assert themselves in the frantic war for big-name guests by issuing an ultimatum that any celebrity, other than the most sought after, caught sitting on Leno's couch might not find a seat on Arsenio's.

According to a former staff member, the ultimatum had come directly from Arsenio. "What he said," the staffer recalled, "was 'I'll take someone second to Johnny, but not Jay.' When someone leaked that to the *New York Post*, though, he backed away and said he'd never said it."

A while later, however, Arsenio made no pretense

of about his desire to be number one with both celebrity guests and ratings.

"I've yielded to Johnny out of respect," he explained to the media, adding, "He's earned it and fought for it for twenty-nine years. I'm happy being the Prince while he is the King. But if you think I'm going to let somebody say, 'Ask Arsenio if I can promote my movie on Skip E. Lowe [host of a public-access interview show in Los Angeles] first,' the answer is 'No, no, no, no, no! No, you can't.'"

Adding fuel to Arsenio's fire was the fact that Helen Gorman Kushnick, Leno's longtime manager who had been named executive producer of "the Tonight Show," had hired Bill Royce, Arsenio's head booker, making him a co-producer and sending him an expensive "Welcome Aboard!" bouquet of flowers on his final day with Arsenio Hall Communications, Ltd.

With his natural distrust of everything and everyone, Arsenio viewed the flower arrangement as an assault upon his kingdom. "Yeah," he had responded, "I've heard the rumors that Jay is coming after me. The other day I was told Jay Leno's camp sent flowers to somebody on my staff to try to lure them away. But I don't worry about that. A talk show is like a big team. You succeed with the effort of each member, unless you're Magic Johnson. Then you realize one guy can be the whole team."

The first sounds of battle rang out when Arsenio was openly contemptuous of Leno in an *Entertainment Weekly* interview, which hit the newsstands only six weeks prior to Carson's departure. I'M GOING TO KICK LENO'S ASS screamed the headline of the magazine's April 17, 1992, cover story a tape-recorded conversation in which Arsenio had nothing kind to say about Leno.

"I hear so many people talking about Jay Leno stepping into Johnny's shoes. I think Jay Leno better just step into a new pair of shoes. He can't replace Johnny. No will ever reign like he reigned. And I think it's an insult to his legacy to say Jay is replacing him. He's done too much. He's been too good. Jay Leno can't replace Johnny Carson. It sounds like an insult."

Adding insult to injury, Arsenio went on to say: "I always hear that Jay and I are friends when they interview him. Jay and I are NOT friends. I think people don't know the definition of the word. I HAVE friends. And I have no problem becoming the friend of a competitor. I would love nothing more than to have dinner with Johnny Carson tonight. I think Dennis Miller's a very bright guy who gets a bad rap—I see him as a nice person. I have no problem saying good things about my competitors, but Jay Leno and I aren't friends.

"No one put the late-night silver spoon in MY mouth. I earned every drop of MINE," Arsenio had continued, adding, "I'm gonna treat him like we treated the kid on the high- school basketball team who was the coach's son. He was there because he was anointed, too. We tried to kick his ass, and that's what I'm going to do—kick Jay's ass. So get ready for me, Jay, and then I'll send you back the flowers you sent here."

"Arsenio got pissed off at Jay because he thinks Jay was handed "the Tonight Show," and that's simply not true," explained a mutual acquaintance. "Jay had done the show for years as guest host. He had a lot of practice."

In point of fact, Jay Leno had been appearing on "the Tonight Show" since 1977. It wasn't until the

1980s, however, that his relationship with NBC fully blossomed, thanks in large part to his many guest appearances on "Late Night with David Letterman."

In 1987, Brandon Tartikoff, who was then NBC entertainment president, tapped Leno for his first— and only—network prime-time special, which earned such high ratings that Leno became a regular guest host of "Tonight" when Carson cut back his taping schedule. It was then, after Joan Rivers had cut her throat with Johnny, that Leno became, as Arsenio would sarcastically point out, the "anointed" successor to Carson.

But the fact that he had been associated with "Tonight" for so many years did not mean that, under his direction, the show was going to remain the same.

"I think Arsenio was caught off guard by the new look and feel of the show once Jay had taken over," confided an acquaintance of Hall's. "Arsenio never understood that Jay was not going to be another version of Johnny and that the show was not going to be a continuation of Johnny's show. He didn't realize that Jay had to play by Johnny's rules as a guest host, but the minute the show became his he would change it, bring it into the nineties."

Arsenio's attack, which had come out of nowhere, left Leno stunned and bewildered, since only three years before, Arsenio had touted him as being one of his few friends. "He taught me a lot about stand-up," Arsenio had stated in a 1989 *US* magazine interview. "A few years ago we used to play this Nintendo game at his house for four or six hours a night. His wife must have absolutely hated me."

That same year Arsenio had described Jay, in a

Time magazine article, as being "pure funny man, more exciting and interesting than Sajak." Of course, he had also humbly added that "Jay's a better stand-up comedian than I am, but when it comes to talk shows, I win hands down."

Arsenio also had been quoted that year in *Rolling Stone,* saying, "Jay Leno's one of the last pure stand-ups left. I love him. But when he got his job with Johnny, I thought that should've been me." Nevertheless, in a May 1989 issue of the *Village Voice,* Arsenio spoke of his friendship with Jay, admitting "I give him jokes and he gives me jokes."

Having first met on the comedy-club circuit in Chicago, the two had been friends since Arsenio had moved to Los Angeles in 1980. They had swapped stories and jokes, spent hours playing Nintendo, and Jay had even taught Arsenio to ride a motorcycle.

Moreover, in 1990, when Arsenio was about to receive his star on the Hollywood Walk of Fame, he had sent Jay a handwritten invitation to the ceremony. "Please come down. It's important you be there," Arsenio had written.

And Jay had been there. In fact, he had been the *only* celebrity on hand to watch Arsenio turn his long-awaited dream into a reality.

"He spent every day at my house for two years," Jay told a TV interviewer not long after the *Entertainment Weekly.* "We worked on material together, went over bits, helped each other out. He brought his mom to my house to meet my wife. When he got a star on Hollywood Boulevard, he made a big deal out of writing me a letter saying it was important to him that I be there. So I just don't understand it," Leno had said, shaking his head in bewilderment.

"This is something we've always wanted to do,"

Leno told a *USA Today* writer shortly before he took over the "Tonight Show" in May. "We thought there'd never come a day when there would be an Italian guy and a black guy hosting talk shows. When you're in competition with someone you like and who's good, it makes better TV all around.

"I consider him an equal," Leno said of Arsenio, adding, "that's what the Constitution says."

Arsenio's response was "We're not really equal. Jay was anointed by Carson and has the backing of a monster network. Regardless of what the Constitution says, inequities in late-night television always exist."

Five days prior to taking over "the Tonight Show," Leno appeared on "Late Night" with Bob Costas and again spoke of his displeasure over Arsenio's attack, which he felt was unwarranted. "The 'kick your ass' thing is okay if you do it in a funny way," Leno said. "The part I didn't like was telling guests if they did "the Tonight Show" they couldn't do his show and that I didn't earn any of this, the way he did."

"What can I say?" an acquaintance of both talk-show hosts rhetorically asked. "Some stars rewrite reality and Arsenio is one of them. The two of them posed for a *Rolling Stone* cover and I know that Arsenio's mother has been to Jay's house on a number of occasions. That sounds like friendship to me."

Ah, but what a strange friendship. When it comes to personality and personal life, Arsenio and Jay Leno are planets apart. Leno has been married to his wife, Mavis, for the past thirteen years. He's a quiet, unassuming guy who, when not on the road doing concerts or club dates, prefers staying home, tinkering with his collection of cars and motorcycles.

Unlike Arsenio, who seems to thrive on discord,

Jay Leno tries very hard not to ruffle any feathers, not to make anyone unhappy, and not to get in involved in controversy. And while Arsenio never leaves home without at least one bodyguard in attendance, Leno travels freely through Los Angeles, accompanied by neither a security guard nor a gun.

The differences also extend their shows. Arsenio rarely mixes with his guests unless they're close friends. Leno, on the other hand, greets each of his guests, either in their dressing rooms or in the renovated "Tonight Show" green room, spending anywhere from five to ten minutes chatting before his brief warm-up of the studio audience.

And there is definitely a difference in their humor, both on and off the stage. For example, two years ago Leno, who was then only a guest host, gave each of "the Tonight Show" staffers a radio in the form of a jukebox as a Christmas present. Hall gave a few of his women staffers a black dildo with an expensive watch wrapped around it, while his other employees received everything from answering machines to white bathrobes with his likeness emblazoned on the back. Both the dildos and the bathrobes were gifts Leno would have considered tasteless.

Although Arsenio later retracted his *EW* attack on Jay, offering the highly unlikely explanation that his statements had been taken out of context in the tape recorded Q & A session, the gauntlet had been flung, the late-night battle engaged.

"It'll be interesting to see what kind of musical sensibilities Jay has," Arsenio confided to his staff. "It'll be interesting to see whether he goes with someone beside him or not, and what he wants to do with the look of the show. If I was him, I'd change my name to John, because I think if it ain't broke, then don't fix it, because you can scare people away. And demographics could start to wander off."

Thus when Leno stepped out from behind the curtain as permanent host of "the Tonight Show" on Monday, May 25, 1992, the winds of war had been blowing through Hollywood for three months. Arsenio, out of deference to Johnny Carson, went into reruns for the first week Leno was on the air. As he would later explain, it was exactly what Carson had done the week he, Arsenio, had debuted.

"Johnny never once jammed me up," Arsenio said. "As a matter of fact, the week I premiered, he took off. That was the ultimate psych. One of the reasons I miss Fred de Cordova [Carson's longtime producer] and Johnny is that these were two of the classiest men in the world—and they were ethical businessmen."

With the battle still raging three months after Leno's ascension to the late-night throne, Dennis Miller, host of the syndicated Tribune late-night show bearing his name, also jumped into the fray after discovering that several of his scheduled guests had canceled at the last minute, supposedly because they'd been strong-armed by "the Tonight Show."

Convinced that his low ratings had been caused, at least in part, by his inability to secure top celebrity guests, Miller lashed out at Leno after he learned that P. J. O'Rourke, the political satirist, had canceled his appearance on the show.

"Dennis got furious about O'Rourkes' cancellation," said a former Miller staff member. "That's when he went on the air and said something to the effect that 'This booking war is ridiculous' and that he didn't care whether a person appeared on his show first or last, but that he didn't appreciate being screwed around like that."

Only a week or two later the Miller show was canceled. Upon hearing this news, Arsenio was on the phone inviting Dennis to be on his show. "He should be staying and punk-ass Leno should be going," Arsenio angrily told his audience, referring to the demise of "The Dennis Miller Show".

"Dennis is a ballsy, honest guy, which is why I respect him," Arsenio said later. "He'll say to your face what he'll say behind our back, and that's very rare in Hollywood".

Annoyed at Leno, now a former "best friend" of Arsenio's from the early eighties, Miller accepted the invitation and appeared on Arsenio's show Monday, July 27, after his show's cancelation the preceding Friday. "Look," Miller said, shortly after this appearance, "I don't even know Arsenio Hall that well. I've met him twice. But he's a legitimate human being who doesn't bullshit you. He's been nothing but classy with me. He's now somebody I want to be better friends with. "Jay and I were very good friends at one point," Miller added, "but I don't think I'd talk to him again, nor would he want to talk to me."

Not long after Miller's appearance on his show, Arsenio confided to friends, "I don't think Leno knows half of the stuff that's going down at his show. Now that all of us are saying these things, maybe we're not so crazy."

"Arsenio may not have enough brains to keep his mouth shut," said a television executive, "but it's been brilliant the way he's used Dennis Miller, having him on his show, touting him on his show. What a joke. Everybody's always known from day one that "The Dennis Miller Show" was a dead duck. Frankly I'm surprised that it lasted as long as it did."

Everyone but Johnny Carson, it seemed, had an opinion about who deserved what in the realm of late-night talk shows as Arsenio continued his assault on Leno. "If you put us both in the Forum, I'd blow him out of the fucking building! It would be like the Lakers versus Hollywood High," Arsenio boasted.

New York shock jock Howard Stern even got into the act when, during a "Tonight Show" appearance on July 24, he lashed out at Arsenio, despite the admonishment of a clearly embarrassed Leno.

"The problem with this show, Jay, is that nobody has any killer instinct," Stern shouted. "He's out to ruin you, this moron who couldn't even do stand-up comedy."

Finally Leno, who prides himself on being Mr. Nice Guy, spoke out. "You know," Leno told the studio audience during his Monday, August 10, 1992, opening monologue, "sometimes people think if people say nasty things about you and you don't answer it, it's a sign of weakness. Well, you don't get this far, you don't get this job, by being weak. And if you don't think nice guys can finish first, just keep watching."

Only a day later Doc Severinsen appeared on Arsenio's show to put in his two cents. "A bunch of screwballs, if you ask me," he said of the new "Tonight Show" cast and crew. "Jay Leno is running around from here to there trying to figure out, 'How can I get them to like me? To watch our show?' And he puts trash on," he told Arsenio, adding that he was appalled by Leno's musical guests. "Frankly,"

Doc concluded, "I haven't seen anything that makes me want to tune in."

Arsenio was ecstatic over Doc's assessment. Not only had Severinsen been a booking coup for his show, he had put down Leno. It was too good to be true.

The reaction at "the Tonight Show" in Burbank, however, was just the opposite. The powers there saw Doc as a traitor. They were especially upset, however, when Ed McMahon also appeared on Arsenio's show. What was particularly upsetting to them was that McMahon apparently had gone on the show with Carson's blessing, since Arsenio screened a rare old "Tonight Show" clip featuring Johnny imitating a dog during an ancient Alpo dog-food commercial with Ed. Everyone knew that Carson owned the rights to the show. Thus the clip had to have his approval to be shown.

Even more embarrassing were the compliments Ed and Arsenio lavished upon each other. Ed presented Arsenio with a specially engraved coffee cup, a duplicate of the ones he and Johnny had used on the set for the thirty years the show had been under Carson's rule.

"Ed's presence on the show," Arsenio later admitted, "meant a lot. It offered a subtext to a lot of people."

It also offered a bit of anguish to the Leno people. "Ed and Doc cut their own throats," confided an NBC executive. "They'll never be invited on the Leno show after appearing on Arsenio. The Leno people saw it as a slap in the face, especially since Jay had personally invited Ed and Doc to be guests on his show.

"I can understand Doc doing Arsenio because he felt the publicity that accompanied Jay's arrival, especially about the show booking younger bands, was saying the old band stunk. He took it as a slap in the face, but it wasn't. It was merely time for a change."

Then, during an interview with Chantal Westerman on ABC's "Good Morning America," the focus of the battle suddenly changed when Arsenio said his argument with Leno was not "professional," it was "personal." "My problem with Jay Leno is not in the late-night arena," Arsenio confided. "I have no problems with Jay as a host or as a competitor. The problem I have with Jay is personal, and that's why I haven't gone into it in detail in the press." However, despite prodding, Arsenio refused to discuss what exactly he meant by "personal."

"We have a personal disagreement," he reiterated to another interviewer several weeks later. "But as far as the talk show, I wish him the best of luck. I have no problem with him as a host."

More confused than ever by this latest revelation, Leno telephoned him. "Arsenio was abusive at first, but then he calmed down and they talked for almost an hour," confided a mutual friend of the two comics.

"Jay asked him, 'What's going on? What do you mean by 'It's personal?' Arsenio told Jay, 'You don't know what's going on? What your staff is doing?' Jay said, 'What are you talking about?' Arsenio kept saying, 'You have to know what I'm talking about.' But apparently Jay didn't because he finally said, 'Think it over and send me a letter.' Arsenio never responded."

Thus, despite the length of the phone conversation nothing was resolved. Even though Jay had sworn he didn't know what Arsenio was talking about, Arsenio was convinced that he did. "When there's a problem, usually you know," he said. Besides, he added, "Something's wrong with someone who's always surprised about people being upset with them."

The battle continued in full public view. In early August 1992, Leno got his chance to take some swipes at Arsenio in his own *Entertainment Weekly* interview. "I understand headline grabbing, but I don't understand the reason for the nastiness of it," Leno said. "The 'punk-ass' thing, how I should have been canceled? All right, but why? I mean, what is this attitude? He makes $12 million a year! Are his monologues worth $9 million a year more than mine?

"What you have here appears to be two million-aires fighting it out. It's fine if it gets more people watching the shows, but why throw rocks at each other. I haven't said anything nasty about him, nor will I. I don't dislike him."

And yet, only a month later, Leno did take a jab at Arsenio and his talk-show style obliquely referring to Bill Clinton who Arsenio tossed barbs at in a monologue shortly afer Clinton had appeared on the show playing the sax. "I watch some other shows," he told an interviewer, "where people trash people, and then they come on and the host says 'You are the greatest!'

"You hypocrite!" Leno said. "If you're gonna make fun of him, at least stand behind it. Branford and I don't do fake high fives. I don't do this 'my man!' stuff. But my proudest thing is that the show crosses all racial lines. It looks like what America looks like."

In September, *Entertainment Weekly* published a letter written to them by Arsenio in response to the magazine's interviews with him and Jay. In his letter, Arsenio took exception to the magazine's implication that his problems with Leno began with their cover story on him. "The problems I've had with Jay date back to the beginning of my show," Arsenio wrote. "As a friend, he would call my office to discuss certain segments of the show he had seen. His calls were always very friendly and complimentary. Yet to other people, Jay would comment very negatively about me and the show. Eventually his views would be repeated to me by our mutual acquaintances and ultimately disclosed publicly through the press."

Citing comments Leno had supposedly made about his performance as a monologist, his level of taste as a talk-show host and the type of guests he booked, Arsenio said he had no problem with Leno's criticisms, but that he did have a problem "with the two-faced approach of someone I had, until that point, called a friend."

The question, of course, is whether or not Arsenio and Leno were ever really friends. Judging from some of Arsenio's past relationships, the answer most likely is no. Since childhood, when he persuaded his playmates to do his bidding, Arsenio has had a talent for creating friendships with people he perceives as powerful or helpful in assisting him to achieve his goals.

Jay Leno was simply one in a long line of people who discovered, after the fact, that Arsenio's prime concern in life is Arsenio. Hall's relentless attack against Leno was more than simply an ego out of control or resistance to anyone, other than himself, taking over "the Tonight Show." It was a visceral response to an ever-present fear of losing, a fear he has never been able to overcome, no matter how much fame, how much fortune he has obtained.

"I am constantly afraid, when a new name comes on the scene, that I'll lose my base," he has often confided to friends. "I thought in the beginning that I was going to create a little niche for myself and just sit back and chill. Now I feel like I'm in a western movie and everybody is coming to town because they've heard about me."

(HAPTER

13

If Arsenio was running on fear in late 1991 and early 1992, it wasn't only because he had misjudged Jay Leno and the new, revitalized format of "the Tonight Show." It was because he knew, as did Paramount, that his once-devoted audience was diminishing and that somehow, someway, he had to replenish it.

In the beginning of his now-four-year run as host of the show, Arsenio had emerged as a hero of Madison Avenue's much-coveted, much-targeted eighteen-to-thirty-four-year-old viewership. It was, in fact, because of these prized demographics that Paramount television had signed him to a new contract, calling for his talk-show services through 1995.

Let Carson and "the Tonight Show" have Middle America and the graying middle-agers, all of whom found Arsenio "too black" for their tastes. The real prize money, at least in advertising revenue, was to be found in Arsenio's target audience—the MTV crowd to whom he was the uncrowned prince of all that was hip, hot, and happening.

Then, in the summer of 1991, for reasons known only to the studio, Paramount Television spent a small fortune with the noted research firm of Frank Magid and Associates on a confidential study of the strengths and weaknesses of "The Arsenio Hall Show".

"They did focus groups, and we sat behind mirrors, and Paramount executives flew in to some cities to listen to people," Arsenio would later explain, adding, "One of the most interesting things that came out of it was that my fans thought that if my competitors and I talked to the same guests, I would get more out of them. "So," he concluded, "as it turned out, the fans were in the opposite direction from all the things the critics had been saying about me since the show began."

Well, not exactly. If Arsenio believed that his fans thought he would get more from interviewing guests than his competitors, he should have read the Frank Magid survey of his audience again. What the Magid report discovered was that "attitudes toward and viewer dependence on 'The Arsenio Hall Show' have softened significantly."

The study went on to point out that the number of viewers who deliberately set aside time to watch Arsenio on a nightly basis had been "cut in half" since the show's debut in January 1989. Based on a telephone survey of more than five hundred late-night viewers, as well as on the series of focus-group interviews to which Arsenio had referred, the Magid survey had found that the number of viewers "who believe the program is outstanding in comparison to others, or offers something unique, is also down sharply.

"Unfortunately," the survey continued, "correcting

these concerns will not be simple. It will not be merely a matter of 'tweaking' the program's pace, set, studio audience participation" because "the problems facing 'The Arsenio Hall Show' are far more fundamental. Viewers simply do not believe the program has the same luster or sparkle it did just a year ago. To many in the audience, the show is just not the 'hip' or 'in' program it once was. Instead, many viewers now see the program as routine and predictable rather than changing and surprising."

As for Arsenio, the Magid study pointed out that Paramount's "primary concern" should be that the show's "youthful core audience" was "not as interested in watching Arsenio Hall himself as it once was" and that "the appeal of seeing Arsenio and his monologue is down quite sharply. The viewers," the report concluded, "seem to feel that Arsenio, like the program, appears tired, bored and perhaps even a little stale."

Magid report had to have been devastating for Arsenio, a man who once laughingly admitted, "I know I come off like Muhammad Ali, but at the same time I'm a very shy, insecure guy. My greatest fear is that my mom and I will be down on the beach selling, 'I Used to Be Busy' T-shirts."

It had to be even more crushing for him to discover that the report had discovered that viewers' opinions of "the Tonight Show" and "Late Night with David Letterman" had remained the same. "Johnny Carson's and Jay Leno's excellent evaluations are unchanged," it stated.

"I'm not surprised by the study, not at all," confided a former Hall staffer. "Arsenio has become very closed off, very greedy, and very spoiled. And he *is* lazy. I remember when the segment producers would go into his office to brief him on that night's guests and he would lay down on his couch, pull his baseball cap down over his eyes, and lie there, with his hands folded. I think that lack of preparation shows on the air. I mean, it's obvious he's not informed about his guests, that he's ill-prepared to do an interview."

Despite the concerns of Paramount executives, however, Arsenio managed to convince them that once Carson had retired and Leno had taken over, he would emerge triumphant because a portion of the viewers would switch to his show.

It was probably around that time, in the summer of 1991, that Arsenio decided, either consciously or subconsciously, to draw attention to the show once Carson announced his retirement by creating a feud between the late-night hosts. What better publicity than that? After all, hadn't his feud with Roseanne made the news? And Madonna? And Spike?

If it all sounded too good to be true, it was. Leno's reputation as a nice guy made him almost impregnable to Arsenio's attacks. And working behind the scenes, Leno's executive producer, Helen Gorman Kushnick, no slouch in the brains department and a fearless warrior for eighteen years on behalf of Leno, quickly moved to seize any power Arsenio might have thought he had in the realm of celebrity bookings.

In the end, of course, Kushnick was removed from her post by the network. By the time she exited the NBC studios in Burbank in October 1992, however, she had left Arsenio in the ratings dust. Having begun a war he could not win, Arsenio ultimately could only offer up the most feeble of reasons for his attack on his former friend Leno in early April.

By late summer, Arsenio seemed to be running

out of steam. "Feelings get hurt and times change, but I have the utmost respect for Jay as an entertainer—so, please, let's move on," he told several inquiring minds from the media.

Although he had put on the gloves and pulled no punches when it came to Leno taking over "the Tonight Show," Arsenio had known, and readily admitted, his syndicated show was out matched in a contest with NBC. "There's too much money and too much inherent power," he had said. "I can't beat the machine. Leno's on a network and I'm in syndication. But my mind-set is that we're going to win. If you shoot for the stars and land on the moon, you're fine."

By the end of summer, however, it had become apparent that he was not going to land on the moon. No matter how fine his aim or how many potshots he fired, Jay Leno was not going to be dislodged from the ratings by Arsenio Hall. In fact, at that point, Arsenio found himself fighting to retain *his* audience as "the Tonight Show" was transformed almost overnight into a hip, musically hot, and topical late-night forum. As a result, it was drawing an increasing number of young viewers, a boon to the NBC network coffers.

"The truth is that 'the Tonight Show' in the last five years was in the low fives in the ratings, a good, solid number, but Madison Avenue felt Johnny had too many over-fifty-five viewers. Jay had to go after a younger audience, whether he wanted to or not," confided a network executive.

And the way to the hearts, minds, and souls of that "younger audience" is to offer musical outings as diverse as the Black Crowes, Simply Red, Garth Brooks, Erasure, and Ricky van Shelton. "I think the booking of the Black Crowes was the first of several devastating blows to him," a former Hall staff member confessed, "because music had always been the backbone of 'The Arsenio Hall Show.' I think it caught him entirely off guard to see Jay booking these musical groups."

Whatever Arsenio's response, by the time summer had given way to fall, it was difficult to tell the two shows apart. Except for their respective hosts, the programs appeared to be edging closer and closer to each other in look, feel, and guests as Arsenio tried to find mainstream America and woo former Carson viewers with guests like Wayne Newton, Olivia Newton-John, Ed McMahon, and Doc Severinsen, while "the Tonight Show" plowed new fields with a far-flung guest lineup of everyone from comedian Billy Crystal to CNN newsman Bernard Shaw to opera star Kathleen Battle.

But despite the verbal jabs, slams, and punches in the ongoing war, the fact remained that with few exceptions, "the Tonight Show" remained comfortably ensconced in the Nielsen upper fives, while Arsenio stayed in third place in the Nielsen threes, tied with the CBS action-adventure series, "Crime After Primetime."

However, since Leno has taken over "Tonight," Arsenio has managed to tie, as well as top, his ratings on several occasions, such as when Madonna appeared on the show in June 1992, and when, two weeks later, Eddie Murphy made a guest appearance to plug his Paramount movie *Boomerang*.

Ironically the Murphy visit earned Arsenio high ratings marks, but it also earned him Eddie's wrath, which is why, only two weeks later, Murphy popped in for a visit on "the Tonight Show" and, during a backstage chat with Leno, was overheard saying, "Arsenio is a two-faced user, man!"

The rift between Hall and Murphy occurred when Arsenio, knowing that his best friend never voted, asked him who he was his choice in the upcoming presidential election.

Murphy, whom Arsenio had introduced as the "Two-Billion-Dollar Man," replied that he trusted in the "higher power" to figure out who would be best to run the country. "Read your Bible," Murphy told Arsenio. "I read Revelations. It don't say nothing about 'Rock the Vote' [commercials by music stars on MTV] aimed at getting youth to the polls."

Unwilling to switch the topic of conversation, Arsenio pressured Eddie about voting, telling him that action as well as prayer was needed. "Eddie was angry," confided an associate. "He felt setup, bushwhacked by Arsenio, who was supposedly his best friend."

And, indeed, months later the two were still not speaking, although by the end of 1992 the tension seemed to have abated, and rumors had begun circulating in Hollywood that the two were discussing the possibility of working together.

With the exception of appearances by Madonna and Eddie Murphy, however, the ratings status quo between Arsenio and his competitors has prevailed. The disaffected Carson viewers, it turned out, did not join Arsenio's home audience. Nor did they take up crocheting. Instead they turned to Ted Koppel and ABC's "Nightline" which, with Carson gone, enjoyed a sudden explosion of viewership and found itself positioned in a very healthy, very solid second-place slot in the Nielsen ratings for that time period.

Once Helen Kushnick was out of the picture, the

war of words between Leno and Hall came to an abrupt halt. Seizing the opportunity, Arsenio claimed that it had been Kushnick's booking practices that had compelled him to speak out. This, he explained, had been his motivation in attacking Leno, first professionally and then, in a sudden change of direction, personally.

"I was telling the press what was going on, and they waited for a white guy named Dennis Miller to say the same thing before they believed it," he explained with the most righteous indignation he could summon up. "They were just saying 'He's the angry black man.' When I said there were classless, unethical things going on, no one said anything.

"My instincts were right, but I was afraid to say what I said. I am a black man in America," he continued, once again aiming one of his extra-long fingers at racist America as if this was somehow connected to his losing fight for ratings.

"It is hard to turn around a country that brought you here to do slave labor," he continued, humbly pointing out, "I was not brought here to be a pop-culture late-night phenomenon. The thing that worried me was I was the first to speak out against this person who smiled on the air and was considered America's Most Beloved. I knew that as a black man in a situation like this, I lose automatically. I'm just happy Dennis got into the fray. Thank God he told the truth about Jay. Otherwise," he concluded, "they'd nail my black ass to the cross."

It was a great speech, but like so much of Arsenio's rhetoric, it had very little to do with reality. The same can be said about his response to a *TV Guide* proposal of a "peace talk" between the two talk-show hosts more than a month later when Arsenio, apparently borrowing a favorite tactic of President Bush, accused the media of protecting his "anointed" adversary.

"Until some of the truth started surfacing, I was in hell," Arsenio wrote in a letter published by *TV Guide* on November 14, 1992. "My fans, as well as the general public, were confused about what was happening. Every time I opened my mouth . . . I was accused of being an angry, jealous liar. I was deeply pained to learn that members of the press would go to such great lengths to protect Leno's golden-boy reputation. "Now," he concluded, "I am trying to close this chapter of my life, though it will never be forgotten."

Arsenio's use of the word "forgotten" was intriguing, especially since he had apparently "forgotten" that it was he, not Leno, who had fired the first salvo long before the booking practices of "the Tonight Show" had become an issue.

CHAPTER
14

Although his feuds with Jay Leno, Spike Lee, Madonna, and Roseanne were essentially fought in the press, several of Arsenio's verbal assaults on other celebrities never really made the news. And that's unfortunate because they offer some revealing insights into the man from Cleveland.

For instance, although he has heaped praise upon Johnny Carson, the supposed architect of his dreams, Arsenio had no compunction in putting Carson down in a 1987 *Cleveland Plaindealer* interview. Carson, he said "should have left [the show] years ago. He's mailing it in. He's very boring."

As for Joan Rivers, the person who gave him not one but two big breaks, he deemed her "too hard to take every night," not long after he had replaced her on the Fox "Late Show" show.

But if Arsenio has a short memory when it comes to the people who offered him a helping hand on his way up the ladder of success, he has a very long memory when it comes to someone he believes has slighted him.

Sonny Bono is a prime example. Apparently Sonny, who chose a political career over show business almost a decade ago, was not deferential enough to Arsenio back in the days when the A-Man was Alan Thicke's answer to Ed McMahon on "Thicke of the Night." Although the show went off the air in 1983, Arsenio still remembers Bono unkindly. "He's not a real nice man," Hall would tell people years later. "I always watched and wondered how the hell he made it."

In a world growing more and more devoid of candor, it can be refreshing to find someone as outspoken as Arsenio. The trouble is that he's become more than simply outspoken. He's become contemptuous and derisive of anyone he believes might be a threat to him or whom he feels has not paid him proper homage.

A prime example of how hell hath no fury like a black talk-show host scorned can be found in Arsenio's digs at Pat Sajak, the fresh-faced host of "Wheel of Fortune."

Arsenio had initially taken a dislike to Sajak when the game-show host once suggested that Arsenio's success was due to his friendship with Eddie Murphy. "Eddie has a lot of friends, but that don't guarantee stardom for them," Arsenio had angrily retorted. "Pat Sajak could be in Eddie's jockstrap and not have a hit show. I get sick of people trying to take the credit away from me as to what I am. I am a blessed, talented, bad motherfucker, and that's why I'm a star."

Another example occured in 1989, only a few days after Paramount had announced they would be producing his forthcoming talk show, Arsenio discovered that his scheduled appearance on the

Letterman show to promote *Coming to America*, had inexplicably been canceled. Tuning in to the Letterman program on this night, he was amazed to see Sajak sitting in Dave's guest chair.

"What bothered me," Arsenio would later confess, "was that Dave was saying to Sajak, 'So, you've got a new talk show coming up against me.' They talked about it, yet they canceled ME out. It would be so easy for me to think it was because I'm black, but that probably wasn't it. Maybe it was because I was perceived as a threat." Since then, Arsenio has remained convinced that Letterman has it in for him. "Dave Letterman hates my guts," he's told people, adding, "Sometimes you're just not somebody's cup of tea."

Arsenio's dislike of Sajak grew even more intense when, only a week after "The Arsenio Hall Show" entered the late-night race, CBS unveiled its first late-night show since the early 1970s . . . a show helmed by none other than Pat Sajak. Arsenio ultimately won that late-night ratings race. But not before he'd trashed Sajak.

"I'm into originals. I watch to learn, and I can't learn from Sajak. He's a very talented guy, but the bottom line is somebody is doing that show already," Arsenio told a magazine writer in early 1989. "Sajak was always a golden boy, though nothing on paper makes him more eligible for that title," Arsenio told another interviewer. "As long as there's an alternative to Sajak, the public will always take it."

Once Sajak's show had disappeared and its host had returned to "Wheel of Fortune," however, Arsenio never mentioned his name again. Why should he? He had won the contest, and Arsenio likes to win. If there's one thing he can't abide it's the thought of being considered a loser, which is one of the reasons he had lashed out at Brandon Tartikoff not long before Tartikoff took over the reins of Paramount Studios. It was a wholly unexpected move, which must have given Arsenio a jolt.

As president of NBC Television, Tartikoff had been quoted in a 1989 *Time* magazine article about late-night television, saying "This race is not a sprint, it's a marathon. Whatever burns the brightest, fades the fastest." He was, of course, comparing the venerable Johnny Carson to newcomer Arsenio Hall. It was a fair comparison, but Arsenio immediately took offense at the remark. "I recently read where Brandon said I was going to burn out fast," he told a reporter, belligerently jumping to his own defense. "Well, I'm not just going to burn bright, Brandon, I'm going to burn long."

A year later, while walking across the Paramount lot, Arsenio encountered Tartikoff, who by then had resigned from NBC and was only a month away from becoming head of Paramount Studios. He took the opportunity to remind his new boss of the *Time* quote.

Tartikoff reportedly listened to Arsenio, with obvious embarrassment, then said, "I was wrong about a lot of things." Turning to one of Arsenio's companions, he then smiled and sheepishly said, "Look, this man outlasted Carson!"

"No," Arsenio responded, "Johnny chose to leave, and I want to continue to play."

Tartikoff had then laughed and invited Arsenio to have dinner with him the following week to discuss future projects. Two days later, however, Tartikoff was quoted in a *Los Angeles Times* article as having described Jay Leno and David Letterman as "the two greatest talk-show hosts in America," aside from Johnny Carson.

"Every time I get ready to sit down and talk to him, I pick up the newspaper and it says, 'Brandon says Arsenio is a jerk-off, a minimal talent, and very lucky,'" Arsenio exploded. "It's like, what do I have to do? I'm the only one who's ever been able to survive the storm of the icon [Carson] and find my own audience. Can't I get a little respect from my partner?"

Arsenio felt humiliated and betrayed, he told friends, by the man who would soon be overlord of the Paramount fiefdom. "I would rather eat the meat off my leg than go to dinner with Tartikoff," Arsenio angrily told associates. "We meet on the lot, and he gives me the black handshake and the whole nine yards. And then I pick up the paper that weekend and read this? And I'm thinking, 'Me and this guy are going to be partners at Paramount?' No way."

But Arsenio Hall didn't rise to his exalted position by chance. According to those who knew him as a college student and as a struggling comic in Chicago, he has always been a genius at selling himself. "He was always aggressive, always manipulative," confided a former Chicago friend. "But you gotta give the guy credit. He made it, big time. And he deserved it. He worked hard at selling himself."

With this in mind, then, it's not surprising that only a couple of days after his Tartikoff tantrum, Arsenio had changed his tune. "I have to talk to Brandon because we're partners, and we need to get together and try to understand each other," he told the people who had been enduring his daily tirades against Tartikoff.

Despite appearances to the contrary, however, the relationship between the two was never more than tenuous at best. For instance, not long after Tartikoff took control of Paramount, he again found himself at odds with Arsenio when the talk-show host, furious that the studio had booked Kim Bassinger and then Harrison Ford on "the Tonight Show", exploded at him over the phone.

According to a former studio executive, Arsenio "went nuts, yelling 'What the fuck are you guys doing to us?' at Tartikoff, pointing out that Paramount was *his* studio and, therefore, should be booking their major movie stars on *his* show."

Six months later, after only fifteen months at Paramount, Tartikoff was gone. He'd resigned his post to be close to his wife, Lily, and daughter, Calla, who was undergoing rehabilitation in New Orleans for head injuries suffered in a 1990 automobile accident.

If Arsenio was pleased by Tartikoff's departure, he didn't express it. For once, Arsenio Hall kept his mouth shut, at least publicly.

Of course, by that time, he'd become embroiled in the yearlong war of words with Jay Leno. Maybe, just maybe, at the time of Tartikoff's departure Arsenio was all talked out. Or perhaps he was too busy reading the writing on the wall, since his talk show had begun faring poorly in the ratings.

Perhaps that's why by the end of 1992, although he had professed to hate making movies only three years before, Arsenio had begun expressing a desire to concentrate more of his energies on producing and starring in theatrical films.

With his show having lost 20 percent of its viewing audience and trailing badly in the ratings, it is more than likely that Arsenio had begun preparing for the possibility that rather than lose money until his contract expired in 1995, Paramount might pull the plug on the show.

This would explain why, as 1992 turned into 1993, he had already begun creating a game plan for the future. "I miss acting," he suddenly announced, not unlike the time he had abruptly confided to Annie Brown that he wanted to be a comedian. "I would swim the English Channel to get an Oscar," he began confiding to friends. "I have an obsession with asking my guests really goofy questions about the Oscars, like 'Where is your Oscar right now?' 'How did you feel when you had it in your hands?'"

Then, in a calculated ploy to explain his drop in ratings should that eventuality occur, he began telling people how he wanted to return to stand-up comedy. "It's so hard for me to do all the things I want to do when I do a show every day. It's an inhuman schedule." Not long afterward, he again returned to the subject of an acting career. "I have been on the cover of *Time*, I have worked the Rose Bowl, I have a star on the Walk of Fame," he told an interviewer. "But the Oscar is some other kind of shit, man."

Thus, it was not coincidental that in August 1992, Paramount announced it would be distributing the first film venture of Arsenio Hall Communications, Ltd., which, with Arsenio as executive producer, would be released in the fall of 1993.

Titled *Bopha* and written by playwright Percy Mtwa, the movie is set in South Africa, circa 1976, during the bloody Soweto uprising, and centers on the lives of a father and son. With Morgan Freeman, the Academy Award–winning actor, making his directorial debut, and a cast led by Danny Glover, Alfre Woodard, and Malcolm McDowell, the film promisesd to provide a classy first effort for Arsenio's company.

By the time *Bopha* was into its final edit, Arsenio had already begun confiding to associates that he had no intention of remaining a talk-show host beyond the limits of his Paramount contract.

"I don't want to be here any longer than my contract calls for," he explained. "I'm not going to be around long enough to hear 'Uncle.' I remember seeing Letterman one night at the Improv, and Bud Friedman said, 'Do twenty minutes, Dave.' He went up and did twelve. He did a funny joke about twelve minutes in, then he said, 'Thanks, and good night.' And he walked out the backdoor, got into his car, and drove away.

"He left us wanting, and I learned something that night. I'm mad at myself for signing for that sixth year. I really want people to say to me one day, 'Why did you leave the show? I really loved what you did.'

"It's like having sex with some girl," he added. "You don't love her anymore but she loves you. You think, 'This is so draining, I don't want to do this.' But you don't know how to tell her it's over. That's the way it is with show business. The feeling has to be there."

But the feeling wasn't there, not like it had been in the past. After almost five years of nightly gabfests, Arsenio often appeared tired of the routine. He was restless, wanting to spread his wings. He still wanted the money and the power a career in show business had brought him, but he'd gradually realized that there were other arenas where his fame and fortune could be utilized and his ego gratified. He could, he concluded, become a kindly benefactor, a force for social change, a power broker on behalf of the powerless.

Thus when his friend Reverend Cecil "Chip" Murray, pastor of the First AME church, had innocently pointed out a crack house blatantly operating across the street from the church one Sunday morning in early February 1992, Arsenio impulsively purchased the ramshackle dwelling. "I bought it because you shouldn't come out of church and see people holding paper bags, walking out through the steel door of a crack house," he explained. "If I had the money, I'd buy them all. Every one of 'em in Los Angeles."

He then wrote out a check for $165,000 to convert the bullet-riddled house into a neighborhood youth center. "I'm going to turn this place into a youth center and I hope to buy more so we can get these drug dealers out of our neighborhoods," he explained. "I hope other entertainers with money will do the same thing. If everyone did, we could wipe out every crack house in L.A."

Three months later, Mayor Tom Bradley officially named July 21, 1992, Arsenio Hall Day and presented him with a shining plaque at a special ceremony "to recognize his compassion and altruism" during the dedication of the transformed crack house. It was a nice tribute to go along with the Key of Life Award he had received from the NAACP during its January Image Awards ceremony for his "work in the crusade for human rights."

"You use what you got to solve the problems that you see," Arsenio told the crowd of well-wishers.

A regular worshiper at the church, Arsenio is known by many of its members as well as by neighborhood residents because he has taken an active interest in the South Central area. To this end he has worked with Reverend Murray in launching a grocery program for the poor and the homeless. In fact, it had been at his invitation that the glamorous all-girl singing group En Vogue had flown in from Oakland to help bag and hand out food to the South Central L.A. residents when the program was launched.

"I can do that," Arsenio had said, referring to what his wealth could buy. "I can feed a thousand people with the drop of a dime. I can just write out a check. That's the cool part of all this."

And when Representative Louis Stokes, a well-known Cleveland Democrat, invited him to appear before a House subcommittee studying violence in America, Arsenio cast aside his fear of flying and gone to Washington, D.C., to testify as the national spokesman of DARE. He had stopped over in Cleveland just long enough to receive an honorary doctorate of humane letters from Central State University and to visit a grade-school class enrolled in the DARE program in nearby Xenia, Ohio.

In Washington, Arsenio entered the House hearing room on April 10, 1992, looking 100 percent Hollywood in a black double-breasted suit, Jet turtleneck sweater, suede shoes, ruby stud in his ear, diamond rings on his fingers, and a diamond gold cross around his neck, his eyes shaded from the flashing bulbs of hovering photographers by wraparound sunglasses. Turning to the standing-room-only crowd in the room, he jokingly asked, "How's everybody?"

In response, a woman noted aloud that "He looks just like himself."

Then, seated in a heavy leather chair, Arsenio tried to break the ice with the subcommittee panel by confessing that he was more nervous at that moment than he had been when walking home as a child after being suspended from school for pulling a girl's hair on the school bus. "This is worse than facing my mother," he quipped, after Stokes introduced him to the committee as a "one-man entertainment machine."

Reading from a prepared statement, Arsenio told the panel: "Violence in this country is destroying the lives of our children and endangering our very future." He cited a 1990 coroner's report from Cleveland listing 221 homicides, 73 percent of them among nonwhite citizens, as members of the Labor, Health and Human Services and Education subcommittee looked on.

After explaining that "some of the homies I grew up with are in jail or dead," Arsenio warned that without a solution, "the next Martin Luther King might not live to adulthood."

Thirty minutes later the hearing ended. Arsenio stepped out into the corridor, popped a stick of gum into his mouth, and let his monster jaw muscles work it over as he walked jauntily away. He had places to go. Children to see. He was on his way to visit a class at George Mason Middle/High School and he was late . . . five hours late, to be exact.

Nevertheless, the youngsters were surprised and delighted when he showed up, especially since he had initially canceled the appearance.

At first flustered by the unannounced arrival of their missing celebrity, the school principal and his secretary had hurriedly called an assembly. Upon entering the auditorium and seeing Arsenio, the students went crazy, barking and waving their arms in imitation of him.

Stepping to the podium, Arsenio quietly waited for

the students to quiet down before delivering his message as the ambassador for DARE. "I wanted to stop by and say that I'm very, very proud of you for having taken part in the DARE program," he told the gathering. "When I was a kid, I didn't have DARE Nobody taught me about drugs. I was from a neighborhood where they sold drugs outside my house, and I had to learn a lot of things the hard way.

"And sometimes, if you don't learn things at a young age, you'll make big mistakes. I was one of those kids from a neighborhood who was told that because I was black, I couldn't succeed. There will be all kinds of stumbling blocks, but I made it against all odds. I made it, and you can make it, too.

"You all are the future. You can make a difference. You can change the world we live in. And I just wanted to stop by today to let you know that I'm not just the guy in that box every night barking. I'm someone who loves you and believes in you."

The moment Arsenio stepped away from the podium, the students sprang from their chairs and rushed forward, thrusting scraps of paper and pencils at him for autographs. With his familiar grin, Arsenio obliged. It was a routine with which he had grown comfortable.

"It's a big inspiration," a teacher explained, watching the action, "because we don't usually have anyone here to build up our kids. When someone like Arsenio comes here and says something, it makes more of an impact because the kids relate to him as part of their culture. He's a positive role model as well as an idol to them."

It was during these forays into the world outside of show business that Arsenio seemed to come alive. He was able to recapture the feeling he had once experienced walking out in front of an audience as a stand-up comic and, later, as the host of his own talk show. It was a feeling that after almost five years of doing talk shows, he had begun to lose.

Less than three weeks after Arsenio returned to Los Angeles from Washington, D.C., a jury of ten whites, one Asian, and one Hispanic returned a not-guilty verdict in the infamous Rodney King beating trial of Sergeant Stacey Koon and Los Angeles police officers Theodore Briseno, Timothy Wind, and Laurence Powell.

The Simi Valley, California, trial had lasted for weeks, but the jury had deliberated only one and a half days before arriving at the verdict, which was delivered at 3:15 P.M. Wednesday, April 29, 1992. The news was greeted with disbelief by the public, most of whom had witnessed the beating on television, thanks to the efforts of George Holliday, who had captured most of it on camera.

Within two hours of the verdict, violence broke out in South Central Los Angeles and quickly spread throughout the city. It was the beginning of what would become the worst riot in the history of the so-called City of Angels. By dark, the Los Angeles skyline was filled with smoke, helicopters, and the flickering embers of a city ablaze.

Concerned about the safety of their workers, all of the networks and studios in proximity to the violence shut down early Wednesday and sent their employees home. The following day, the city issued a dusk-till-dawn curfew, which was not lifted until the following Sunday evening.

Since Paramount is located in the heart of Hollywood and, by Thursday, was in the path of the looters and arsonists, Arsenio was told he would have to shut his show down and go into reruns until order could be restored in the city.

"Brandon Tartikoff called me and said that we were not doing a show," he later recalled, "but I said 'Oh, no . . . we doin' a show.' There were two days left to go in the week, Thursday and Friday, and I told him I'd take one. Don't get me wrong. He was being intelligent. He had to consider the insurance, the violence. He told me that if anybody got hurt, I would not be a hero, I'd be an idiot. And he was right.

"The Sears store on Santa Monica was burning," he continued. "You could see the smoke, smell it in the air. People were afraid to come out, so I bused in people from my church to be my audience.

"My thinking was there were people at home watching TV, there was a curfew, and it was important to open up a dialogue," he said, explaining, "One of our biggest problems is we don't know each other and we don't talk."

So even though he realized Tartikoff was right, Arsenio refused to cancel the program's Thursday-night taping. As he explained later, "I came into my dressing room after taping the show that first night of the riots, and when I turned on the TV," he said, "one of the looters was wearing a Martin Luther King T-shirt. It seemed like the ultimate irony. So I told Marla, my producer, 'Let's open the show with Martin Luther King and the words that would be appropriate to the unrest.'"

Thus the only sign of life on the Paramount lot that night was on Stage 29, where Arsenio sat on a barstool, wearing a cool, green double-breasted suit, talking to Mayor Tom Bradley, who had agreed to appear on the show despite the violence and the fact that he had not slept for more than a day at that point.

"I called and called Mayor Bradley," Arsenio said. "I was not going to take no for an answer. He was very busy, but as soon as I got him on the phone, the first and only thing that came out of his mouth when he heard what I wanted was yes."

The message of that evening was very simple, very straightforward. "This is the time for every black man and woman to know where your sons and daughter are—spend time talking, watching TV, eating, whatever—'cause if you don't, you may find them in the grave," Arsenio told his audience.

Later, after the show had been taped and sent to the station affiliates via satellite, Arsenio canceled his plans to fly to the Kentucky Derby in Louisville. Instead of cheering rapper M. C. Hammer's horse, Dance Floor, at Churchill Downs, Arsenio had decided to volunteer his services to the riot-torn South Central community.

So immediately after the taping, he accompanied comedian Sinbad and actor Edward James Olmos to the AME Church for a discussion with community leaders of ways to encourage people to be peaceful in their protest. "I have to do something," he said at the time. "It's not a black-white thing. There are white people who are outraged, too. It's wrong to try to solve the problem with violence."

During the ensuing days, Arsenio was a whirl-wind of activity. He dedicated both his Thursday- and Friday-night shows to a pursuit of peace and followed Mayor Bradley's Thursday-night appear-ance with a Friday-night visit from the Reverend Jesse Jackson. He visited the riot's first victim, truck driver Reginald Denny, in the hospital. And he worked at the church, helping to distribute food to riot victims.

And to critics who dared to suggest he might be out of his element by temporarily turning his nightly format of celebrity chat, comedy, and music into a political forum, he replied: "The party is still at my house, but sometimes the music stops. Sometimes there's meaningful conversation. You learn things. You get informed and you meet new people.

"It's my house and I decide every night who I'm going to invite," he said, confiding, "Right now I'm so worried about my country that I'm interested in talking to politicians."

It was not long afterward that Arsenio invited Bill Clinton to be a guest on his show. George Bush's post-riot visit to Los Angeles, on the other hand, only earned him Arsenio's disgust.

"What can I say? I spent a lot more time in the neighborhoods he shot through in a limo, and I'm very angry. I know comedians aren't supposed to be angry, but I'm very angry."

Despite his meteoric rise within the television industry and on the Paramount back lot, Arsenio has always placed himself outside the crowd and, therefore, felt far removed from the inner workings of the Hollywood entertainment industry. It is a system he deems superficial and labyrinthine.

"I haven't gotten used to it," he's often said of the two-faced style of business that permeates the corridors of Tinseltown. "And," he added, "I don't think I should get used to it. That's why I keep to myself.

"If you get close to it," he continued, "it's just going to cause you pain. So I keep to myself. I'm able to insulate my world, and I know it's all right there. I know I can trust everybody who will come into my house. So I just put up a wall and stay inside it."

He had gone into the business distrustful of all he surveyed, and nothing he had seen or experienced had diminished that distrust. The controversies, the lawsuits, the supposed betrayals, the politics of the business had all served to increase his paranoia. If anything, he confided, he was more distrustful than ever.

"This business has changed me," he admitted not long ago.

"I trust people less. I understand now that my manager is just a business partner and that he's here to get paid if it means walking over my body to get the check. And the affiliates aren't my friends. It's all just business.

"I very rarely meet people who don't want something," he added, ignoring the fact that he was once a member of that same club. "Most of the people who are around me and close to me are on salary," he continued. "You'd be surprised at how many people wouldn't give you the time of day if there wasn't a check involved."

Those were sad words coming from someone who had traveled so far, so high, so fast to achieve his version of the American Dream. In only three short years, Arsenio had used his boyish charm, his zealous embrace of young talent, his irreverent humor, his natural curiosity and devil-may-care attitude to become the hippest host ever to grace the late night airwaves.

"I came along and did something I don't think anybody else thought could be done," he once rightfully proclaimed. "Twenty-three people challenged Johnny and tried to play him on his home field. Then I came along and said, 'Isn't there someone who doesn't watch him? Don't they need a show?' It was as simple as that. It wasn't a stroke of genius."

By mid-1992, Arsenio had become entranced with his status as a positive role model and outspoken critic of America's social ills, especially those related to the black community. He had elevated himself from a mere TV talk-show host to a major influence peddler, who could pick up the phone and talk to just about any noteworthy person in the nation—with the obvious exception of George Bush and his staunch Republican followers, who would not soon forget his on-air tirade against their leader.

People sought him out. People believed in him. People listened to him. And the more they listened, the more Arsenio talked, offering his opinions on every conceivable topic—from his talk-show competitors to condoms to civil rights to drug abuse to the evils of lip-synching, as in the Milli Vanilli case.

"I am," he declared, "America's most schizophrenic entertainer. One day I have a heart of gold. The next day I want to march with Al Sharpton the rest of my life."

People who have come to know Arsenio as a shallow user of others give little credence to his supposed commitment to social change. They see his good works as merely one more ego trip, one more testimonial to his ability to hide behind a mask of self-righteousness.

In the opinion of one former friend and confidante, "He plays up to black people, but in his heart he's not black. And the black community knows it. They think he's an Uncle Tom. They know he goes out with a lot of white women. They know all about him, and a lot of black people just don't like him."

But to the average black person, young and old, Arsenio Hall has become someone to admire, someone who has played the mainstream game of white

America and has somehow managed to win the contest on his own terms. In doing so, he has managed to become a symbol of the American Dream, bringing hope to those who have lost it and offering faith for a better tomorrow to those who can barely make it through today.

Whatever the wellsprings of his generosity, whatever the authenticity of his newly found social stance, he has devoted his time, energy, and money to better the lives of his fellow African Americans, which is more than many other young black stars of his stature have done.

For those reasons, in spite of his imperfections and his "do as I say not as I do" dual life, Arsenio Hall deserves credit for not only turning his dream into a reality, but for inspiring other people to dream, too. Prevaricator extraordinaire that he is, Arsenio managed to succeed where everyone else, black and white, had failed. And in doing so, he blazed a trail into unknown turf with a style, sometimes even a grace, that was totally his own.

"You can try to be liked by everybody," Arsenio once explained. "You can kiss a lot of ass and step on no toes and make a good living, but that's not the route I've chosen to take. I'll take mine and I'll take the hate because when it's all over, I don't want to just leave a legacy of Chapstick on the back of people's pants."

Welcome to the world of Arsenio Hall, Chapstick and all.

He created it. He resides in it. He reigns supreme in it. And, ultimately, he will either flourish or perish in it.

Aileen Joyce is the pseudonym of a full-time writer and the author of *Michael Landon: His Triumph and His Tragedy*. This is her first book for HarperPaperbacks.